SpringerBriefs in Eco

C000000829

More information about this series at http://www.springer.com/series/8876

June A. Sekera

The Public Economy in Crisis

A Call for a New Public Economics

 Springer

June A. Sekera
Global Development and Environment
    Institute
Tufts University
Somerville, MA
USA

ISSN 2191-5504   ISSN 2191-5512   (electronic)
SpringerBriefs in Economics
ISBN 978-3-319-40486-8   ISBN 978-3-319-40487-5   (eBook)
DOI 10.1007/978-3-319-40487-5

Library of Congress Control Number: 2016943383

This Springer imprint is published by Springer Nature
The registered company is Springer International Publishing AG Switzerland

Acknowledgements

This book would never have happened were it not for opportunities opened for me by a series of people. After reading my working paper on economics and the public economy, Charles Hall, a pioneer in the emerging field of biophysical economics, identified me as a kindred spirit; it was he who suggested that the paper could be the basis for a book and introduced me to Springer. That working paper itself would never have happened were it not for Neva Goodwin, the courageous economist who was first to comprehend my argument and vision, and who could see its connection to her pathbreaking work on the "core economy." And nothing would have happened at all were it not for Hillel Schwartz, who inspired me to take up the challenge of writing about what I know, and whose rhetorical and editorial talents immensely improved upon my too-often pedestrian prose.

I also thank Michael Bernstein for putting me in touch with Edward Fullbrook, who provided the initial platform for my early consideration of public goods. Subsequently, I have been fortunate to have had the intellectual support of Jonathan Harris, Victoria Chick, Merijn Knibbe, and Kent Klitgaard, from whose insights I continue to benefit, as I have from conversations and exchanges with Frank Ackerman, Roger Backhouse, Ron Baiman, Fred Block, Will Davies, Charlie Derber, Bill Domhoff, Jerry Friedman, Julie Froud, Nance Goldstein, David Hall, Will Hatcher, Inge Kaul, Steve Keen, Ted Lane, Steve Marglin, Bill Moomaw, John Mills, Claus Offe, Avner Offer, Christopher Pollitt, Stewart Ranson, Brian Roach, Sam Rosenberg, Cheryl Thomas, John Weeks, and Burton Weisbrod.

Contents

List of Figures

Introduction

Public non-market production makes up a quarter to a half or more of all economic activity among advanced democratic nation-states. Yet the public economy's ability to function on behalf of the populace as a whole is seriously imperiled in many Western democracies and particularly jeopardized in the USA.

This Brief concerns the nexus between mainstream, market-centric economics, and what James Galbraith (2008) has called "the collapse of the public governing capacity." That collapse is due in great measure to the imposition of market precepts on the public domain. Marketization and its confederates, privatization and profitization, have led to the evisceration of governmental capacity, the downsizing of democracy and the dismantling of traditions of responsible public administration grounded in law and constitutional government.

Political science gives us a theory of popular sovereignty wherein "The People" is the sovereign, and power emanates from the people through a constitution to the organization we call "government." In effect, the theory of popular sovereignty creates a collective sovereign. To carry out the will of the collective sovereign, government must produce goods and services. If political science predictably ignores this function of production in the public domain, remarkably so does contemporary mainstream economics. The current "public economics" and "public choice" schools seem at first glance to treat seriously the public non-market economy only to default to inadequate conventional theory, inappropriate analytical approaches, or inapplicable market axioms.

Government produces its outputs in a non-market environment. Its resource inputs are supplied collectively: from the authority of the people (their votes for elected representatives) and from their aggregate financing (taxes). The intent and the result of government's collective-choice, collective-financing system of production is that goods, services, benefits, and protection are supplied for the well-being of the society as a whole, and can be accessed regardless of personal wealth because they are provided free or below cost at the point of usage. Economic theory today lacks any cogent theory of this non-market environment.

Indeed, a myopic market-centric view of the public economy prevails in text-books, in university classrooms, in the documents and debates shaping public policy, and in the current practice of public administration.

Moreover, there is no consensus within public administration practice or scholarship about how to assess results or measure outcomes in the public domain. Nor does economics concern itself with the pragmatic aspects of outcomes measurement in distinctly non-market environments. Given this void, a corporate model of performance measurement has been imposed on the public domain, where market-mimicking values and purposes displace public purpose in measurement schemes. The consequences of this contrived and contorted imposition range from the unfortunate to the disastrous.

Public administration has been molded (or deformed, say many observers) by the so-called New Public Management (NPM), "a child of neoclassical economics" (Osborne 2006). NPM has colonized and weakened every level of government. My brief details how the axioms of mainstream economics have been the driving force behind the debasement and destruction—sometimes unintentional but often intentional—of the public governing capacity. Agencies originally created to meet a public need are being warped into entities whose purpose is to generate revenue and, in some cases, deliver private profits at public expense.

Hollowed out through the cathartic of a "competition prescription" (Kettl 1993), the public sector begins to fail. Systems of performance measurement are then put in place, ostensibly to improve results but instead often leaving harm in their wake. While government "reinventors" boast about shrinking government, in reality a shadow government has mushroomed, with an explosion of private contractors reaping taxpayer-funded profits. We find our most basic public services and rights in jeopardy, from clean air and water to unencumbered judicial due process.

Lacking a coherent concept or understanding of how the public non-market actually functions, reformers dedicated to a vibrant democracy and effective government are denied a viable foundation on which to restore and revitalize public sector capabilities.

More than a century ago, the effective operation of the public economy was a significant, active concern of economists. With the rise of market-centrism and rational choice economics, however, government was devalued, and its role circumscribed and seen from a perspective of "market failure." As Backhouse (2005) has shown, the transformation in economic thinking in the latter half of the twentieth century led to a "radical shift" in worldview regarding the role of the state. The very idea of a valid, valuable public non-market has almost disappeared from sight.

Writing about the theoretical foundations of the attack on government, Stretton and Orchard (1994) stressed the need for theory as "intellectual equipment" with which to combat the assault. McGarity (2013a, b) argues for a new "idea infrastructure" to rebuild ravaged public administrative capabilities. In *The End of the Experiment?* Bowman et al. (2014, p. 143) observe that we live in "a political economy that generates the conditions for its own failure." Confined and constrained by an overarching premise of market superiority, "the state lacks basic conceptual tools to think differently" (p. 131).

It is time to stop squinting at the public sector through a market lens and to see public production as a distinct, valid economic process. It is high time that we seek, and arrive at, an understanding of how the public non-market works. Only then will it be possible to appreciate how intrinsically and crucially different are the dynamics of the public non-market from those of the market. At that point, we can establish operational methods of governance that produce desired results.

We need a new approach to public economics.

Toward that end, this brief sketches the elements of a theory of the public non-market and illuminates its connections to the delegation of power and the collective provision of resources from the polity.

In the public non-market, the most basic constructs of mainstream economics do not apply. There are no "buyers," no "sellers," and no "exchange." There is no market-model competition, only "pseudo-privatization" (Siltala 2013). The driver is not demand but identified societal need. Satisfying "customers" does not produce revenue. The monopsonist is often rendered powerless to set prices. Government expenditure actually results in "crowding-in," boosting rather than curtailing growth. In a non-market, outcome goals are devilishly difficult to define—unlike the simple market goal of maximizing profit. Results are often obscured because of factors unique to non-markets, where *invisibility* of outputs and *absence* of harmful conditions are hallmarks of success.

Woefully lacking is an economics that reflects upon and draws its explanatory power from the fact that it is the people whose sovereign collective authority and aggregate resources animate and supply the public non-market. We must also make evident the intimate connection between economic thought and public administration. As things stand now, public administration *practice* is contextualized within, and controlled by, market-centric, neoclassical economics, while public administration *theory* avoids economics like a plague.

A new, cogent and catalyzing public economics can inform and improve public administration while helping to rebuild the machinery and restore the capabilities of government. Citizens of democratic nation-states must recognize that public products originate from the polity itself, that well-being requires vigilant guarding of the public purse, and that choice and accountability are at the ballot box.

Chapter 1
"Government Is Broken": The Collapse of the Public Governing Capacity

Contemporary mainstream economics has been a prime factor in the degradation of the public governing capacity in the United States and other western democracies. The marketization of American government, in particular, is the chief reason for its declining ability to reliably deliver goods and services. Market advocates, exploiting neoclassical economic theory, have transformed public goods production in imitation of a market model. This has led, sometimes intentionally, to the evisceration of public services and the dismantling of traditions of responsible public administration. Democratic, constitutional governance is threatened. The ravaging of government in the interests of ideology or private profit has proceeded largely unhindered because we have no adequate theory to explain the roots and express the essential value of the non-market public economy, no intellectual infrastructure to explain how its purposes and processes differ crucially from those of the market, and no effective conceptual model that demonstrates why such differences matter substantially for democratic governance and for the well-being of the citizenry.

Although this Brief focuses on the United States, essentially the same incapacitation of government has been taking place in other western democracies–Canada, Australia, New Zealand, the UK, and in parts of continental Europe, and is being exported to developing countries. While the contagion arguably arose simultaneously with the Reagan administration and Thatcher government during the 1980s, since then the U.S. has been its chief breeding ground.[1]

---

[1] With respect, for example, to the assault on British public universities, Simon Head (2011) has described how the siege of the public sphere is part of an "American zeitgeist" of corporatization: "The theories and practices that are driving this assault are mostly American in origin, conceived in American business schools," and transplanted elsewhere, he writes, by way of management consulting firms.

© June A. Sekera 2016
J.A. Sekera, *The Public Economy in Crisis*,
SpringerBriefs in Economics, DOI 10.1007/978-3-319-40487-5_1

"Government Is Broken"

There is a widespread belief in the United States that government is broken, especially at the federal level. A sampling of headlines: "Why Government Fails So Often" (Schuck 2014); "Saving America from Broken Government" (Howard 2014); "Over half of Democrats say government is broken" (Smith 2014); "Where Government Falls Apart" (Fahrenthold 2014); "'Washington Is Broken,' Polls Say Americans Say" (Luntz 2014). Some point to legislative gridlock, others to the growing inability of government to deliver intended results. My concern is with the latter, although I disagree with those who blame innate administrative incompetence,[2] "the kludgeocracy" (Teles 2013) or the "virus of cynicism" (Bruni 2014).

Mainstream economic theory, with its market centrism and its dismissiveness of "the state," provides too-ready ammunition for those who claim that government is intrinsically ineffective and inefficient. The axioms of the "public choice" school, in particular, suggest that government incompetence is innate. But there is another explanation, not often heard.

James Galbraith (2008) is one of the few who offer an alternative, and cautionary, view. Writing about the "collapse of the public governing capacity," he made it clear that the erosion of state capability was neither innate nor incidental; rather, it was the result of a purposeful, systemic campaign by private interests to "suck the capacity from government and deplete it of the ability to govern." He warned that inadequate attention had been paid to the deliberate dismantling of the machinery that enables the state to produce for the common good.

Claus Offe, a political sociologist at the Hertie School of Governance in Berlin, also warns that we ignore at our peril the degradation of the machinery of the state. In an essay on "Shared Social Responsibility" (Offe 2014), he observes that "Despite our dissatisfaction with the inadequacies of public policy, we should not forget that the democratic state and its powers to tax, spend and regulate remains the major instrument for sharing responsibility among members of society" (p. 8). And he argues, in opposition to the markedly individualist strains of market orthodoxy, that "The democratic state, in spite of its limitations, remains—or must be restored to its role as—a key strategic agent both in containing the negative externalities of individual choice and creating and implementing collectively binding solutions" (p. 9).

Unfortunately, strategies for governmental reform in the U.S. over the last decades have relied consistently on the creed of market superiority, as if the cause could be the cure. Writing shortly after the Clinton administration rolled out its "Reinventing Government" initiative, public policy scholar Donald Kettl neatly summed up the approach, previously a hallmark of the Reagan administration: "The theory of the market is at once an explanation of what is wrong and what can be done to make things right…The federal government's usual approach is to assume that the market knows best" (Kettl 1993, pp. 2, 182).

---

[2]"Corruption" is also blamed. But that is not my topic. Moreover, corruption is simply another term for private interests replacing the public interest. Cf. Teachout (2014).

So the solution to "broken government," both for those wanting to shrink government and those hoping to make it work better, has been to refashion government in the image of the market, either by contracting out its work or by transplanting commercial (business) values and practices onto what was left.[3] As I will detail, when marketization is the preferred method of reform—regardless of motivation—the result is disabled government.

One of the most compelling aspects of Galbraith's work is his perception of how entrenched the creed of market superiority has become, such that government administrators now routinely try to apply "a market solution where markets had never existed" (p. xii). Indeed, mainstream economic thinking has carried market-mimicry into ever-widening spheres of the public domain, where public university students and hospital patients alike are being re-branded as "customers." As Galbraith tells us, there is virtually no counteraction because "respectable opposition demonstrates fealty to the system by asserting allegiance to the governing myth [of market superiority]. This in turn limits the range of presentable ideas, conveniently setting an entire panoply of reasoned discourse beyond the pale of what can be said, at least in public…There is a process of internalization, of self-censorship. Once the rules and boundaries prescribed by the myth are understood, adherence becomes reflexive, and at the end of the day, people come to think only what it is permitted to think" (pp. xvii–xviii).

The encroachment has been gradual but pervasively and perversely effective. Subscription to market principles is not only demanded by prevailing norms within the halls of government; it goes unquestioned. Speaking from my three decades of experience in developing policy, managing programs and agencies, and program evaluation and performance measurement[4] at the federal, state, and local levels of government, I can attest that the prevailing creed since the 1990s stifles reasoned discourse among government leaders, managers and employees. There has been a continual hollowing-out and a loss of institutional knowledge about alternatives, what Kettl calls a "national amnesia." The prevailing economic creed drives every aspect of the practice of public administration, which, in a vicious circle, further undermines governmental capabilities.

A Theory of Public Incompetence

The market-centrism of mainstream economics has played directly into political and popular media views of government as incompetent and inefficient.

---

[3]Recently, several new public administration theories have offered alternative prescriptions. As I shall discuss in Chap. 3, these have neither engaged with the fundamental problem of a flawed economic model, nor have they been put into general practice.

[4]In the fields of workforce training, adult education, economic development and employee ownership.

In *Public Goods, Public Enterprise, Public Choice*, Stretton and Orchard (1994) analyzed four beliefs that together constitute "a theory of public incompetence."(p. 80) All four derive from the axioms of neoclassical economics, in particular that self-interest is the universal motivator, and that markets, unlike governments, are invariably efficient, punishing failure by eliminating inefficient producers.[5]

Much earlier, Studenski (1939) brilliantly described and disputed the "theory of nonproductivity" of government, which formed "a fundamental tenet of the so-called classical and neoclassical schools of economics still dominant in this and many other countries…" One passage (pp. 23–24) is worth quoting at length.

Theory of Nonproductivity

Towards the end of the eighteenth century…under the influence of the industrial revolution, a sudden revulsion took place in the political and economic thinking of the time. The entrepreneurial class, in its quest for freedom from restrictive governmental regulation, attacked the ability of government to attend to the economic affairs of its citizens. Political economists took the view that business enterprise was the sole productive agency in society and that government was a passive, nonproductive, wealth-destroying organization…

Strange as it may seem, this peculiar doctrine of the nonproductivity of government activity has tended to persist to the present day, and forms a fundamental tenet of the so-called classical and neoclassical schools of economics still dominant in this and many other countries at the present time. The theory of the nonproductivity of government activity is founded on several basic errors, to wit: (1) a tendency to regard government as an organization independent and apart from the people and pursuing its own advantage; (2) a wrong identification of economic activity with individual endeavor to make a living, and a failure to recognize the importance of collective economic effort; and (3) an unduly narrow commercial view of production as the creation of utilities having an exchange value. The exponents of the nonproductivity theory of government activity fail to see that government in modern democratic society, with which we are particularly concerned, is an agency set up by the people for their own advantage and controlled by them with a view thereto, and is, in fact, in some of its aspects, the people themselves acting collectively. Quite erroneously they conceive of government as being operated for the sole advantage of scheming politicians. It is wrong to conceive of economic effort as being purely individual in character. Under all forms of organized society, economic activity has required some collective effort in addition to the individual one, and this is still true of the modern society. The notion that production for exchange is alone "productive" is preposterous. [Emphasis added]

Seventy-five years later, in a similar vein, Paul Krugman (2014b) would address "the incompetence dogma" and "how completely ideology has trumped evidence" about government, making "rational analysis of policy issues impossible."

---

[5]The rise of rational choice theory after World War II has been a major factor in the devaluing of government and its de-legitimization as an economic actor, as I discuss in Chap. 6.

Government Isn't Broken (Yet), (Though the Incompetence Dogma Reigns)

Despite the barrage of headlines telling (sometimes falsified) stories of government failures, in reality government succeeds far more often and far more widely than it fails. The successes, however, go largely unseen or unacknowledged, for reasons I shall soon discuss.

David Leonhardt (2014), reviewing one of many books about government failure, will tolerate neither the dogma nor the blindness: "If you wanted to bestow the grandiose title of 'most successful organization in modern history,' you would struggle to find a more obviously worthy nominee than the federal government of the United States. In its earliest stirrings, it established a lasting and influential democracy. Since then, it has helped defeat totalitarianism (more than once), established the world's currency of choice, sent men to the moon, built the Internet, nurtured the world's largest economy, financed medical research that saved millions of lives...".[6]

In a book that challenges the dogma of incompetence, Charles Goodsell (2014; cf. Lipsky 2014) shows how American government has performed both complex and routine tasks efficiently and effectively. And Allan Rosenbaum, a professor of public administration and recent past-president of the American Society for Public Administration, has directly taken on "the myth of public sector failure and incompetence," pointing to such achievements as the construction of our national system of superhighways and statewide public higher education. Government hasn't failed, he writes (Rosenbaum 2014b, p. 3), but public administrators have— in "being hesitant to speak of the central importance of what we are about boldly, loudly and effectively," while "practitioners in the private sector and business school faculty glorify the power and creativity of the American private sector."

Why, for example, are we not hearing more about how public investment in technology produced the innovations that led to the iPhone (Mazzucato 2013), or how major corporations harvest and profit from the crop of successful innovations (Lohr 2012) that grow from publicly-funded research?

And why must we turn to the obscure *Federal Computer Week* (Lutton 2014) to learn that "Top e-government websites–specifically those of the Social Security Administration and the Department of Health and Human Services–often outrank top private-sector sites from the likes of Amazon, Apple and FedEx for customer satisfaction"?

All together, writes James Galbraith (2008, p. 112), federal government pro-grams for health care, higher education, housing and Social Security account for nearly 40 % of total consumption of goods and services in the U.S. "Taking everything together, we find that the United States is not a 'free-market' economy

---

[6]For more on the vast array of government's accomplishments and successful economic pro-duction, see Lind (2012) *Land of Promise*, and see Hacker and Pierson (2016) *American Amnesia* on how the collective memory of those accomplishments has been erased.

with an underdeveloped or withered state sector. It is rather, an advanced postin-
dustrial developed country like any other, with a government sector responsible for
well over half of economic activity."[7]

While the ideological imposition of market models has increasingly disabled
government (see my Case Examples below), it is the myth of market superiority that
has shrouded the major contributions of government to national well-being.

The Lack of Conceptual Tools to Think Differently

In order to restore the full effectiveness of government in meeting public needs, the
entrenched myth of market superiority must be countered and replaced with a valid
theory and model of the non-market public economy, one that recognizes and
explains government-as-producer.

A few recognize the need. Stretton and Orchard (1994) stress the importance of
theory as "intellectual equipment" with which to combat the contemporary attack
on government. McGarity (2013a) argues for a new "idea infrastructure" to rebuild
depleted public administrative capabilities.[8] "The state lacks basic conceptual tools
to think differently," say the British authors (Bowman et al. 2014, p. 131) of a
recent book about the doxic, market-centric frame that controls public
policy-making in the UK and the US.

Useful public sector reform has been thwarted for many reasons, among these
the reluctance of public administration theorists to engage directly with the economics behind the marketization of government. Beryl Radin, an eminent scholar of
public administration, calls attention to the distance between theory and practice in
the field, which has "moved along two separate tracks—one attached to the
experience of practitioners and one attached to more traditional academic settings
accentuating theory rather than practice," (Radin 2012, pp. 11, 16) Nowhere do
theorists of public administration adequately attend to the concept of non-market as
an alternative to the market-centric norm determining actual practice.

One purpose of this Brief is to trace the baneful influence of the values and
principles of mainstream, market-centric economics on the current *practice of
public administration*—and in so doing to demonstrate the seriously dark consequences that follow from the absence of a coherent, valid theory of how the public
non-market works. Crucially missing from economic thinking as well as from the
principles and practice of public administration is an understanding of the forces
and dynamics of the public non-market production economy. Lacking a valid
theory or cogent model, we have no sturdy intellectual equipment on the basis of

---

[7]Galbraith's estimate of "over half" includes health care, higher education, housing, Social
Security, and "nonmilitary public expenditures at the federal, state and local levels," of which a
large part is public K-12 education.

[8]McGarity offers a cogent and extensive argument for an "idea infrastructure" meaning new
visions and concepts to support the restoration of "robust institutions" of governmental protection.

which to counter theoretical and actual attacks on government and restore its capacity to operate effectively on behalf of all citizens. In Chap. 5, I outline the dynamics and forces of the public economy that are not adequately addressed, let alone explained, by mainstream economics.

Professor Luiz Carlos Bresser-Pereira (2014), former Minister of Public Administration for Brazil, asks: "Why don't we have a literature discussing the relations between public managers and economists?" Another aim of this paper is to reclaim and foster such a relationship, which a century and more ago had been nurtured by late-19th-century European writers on "public finance" (Backhouse 2002, p. 166; Caldwell 2005, pp. 42–43). That relationship was derailed by the juggernaut of market-centric economics that views public production as a glaring symbol of market failure.

NOTE: This Brief will not discuss the myriad flaws of the market model or the ways the model has been challenged by heterodox and pluralist economists. Nor will it delve into the ways in which the market cannot, in fact, operate without government. These topics have been extensively argued and documented elsewhere. My argument concerns the *absence* of a valid theory of the public non-market economy, and my aim is to begin to suggest the elements of such a theory.

Terms Used in This Brief

The terms "privatization," "marketization," and "outsourcing" are often used interchangeably, with definitions that differ by continent and discipline. Here is how I use the following terms:

Privatization. Outside the US, particularly in Europe and Anglophone countries, privatization means the selling of a publicly-owned physical asset or organization, with ownership and operation transferred to the private sector. In the US (and as I use it in this Brief), the term privatization has a different meaning: (1) the contracting-out (or "outsourcing") of the operation of a public service, without transferring ownership, and/or (2) enabling a private sector organization, through other methods, to operate a public asset or deliver a public service at public expense. In both cases the private contractor gains financial benefit (profit) from the service operation or delivery. Privatization in the U.S. also comes in other guises, such as "public-private-partnerships," "innovative financing methods," and "social impact bonds".

Contracting out (or "outsourcing"). A sub-category of privatization in which the government pays a private company to undertake a function previously performed by government employees.

Public non-market economy. The economy in which goods, services and other products are paid for collectively (through taxes) and which, in a democratic nation-state, are originated through collective choice (voting). I explain the concept further throughout the paper.

Marketization. The imposition or infusion of market values, principles or practices on public (government) non-market operations, whether directly-operated or contracted out. The marketization of government operations that are staffed directly by public employees is largely invisible to those outside government, and is a principal concern of this Brief.

Pseudo-market. This term underscores the misconception that when market values and market-mimicking practices are imposed upon the public non-market domain, a market environment (and its alleged benefit) arises. That is not the case (see Chap. 4). The term "pseudo-market" is a more accurate descriptor of the environment in which marketization and privatization (contracting-out), occur.

Pseudo-privatization. This term, which I borrow from Juha Siltala (2013), counters the illusion that contracting-out introduces the supposed virtues of the market, such as efficiency and cost-effectiveness, by giving rise to "market mechanisms" and market dynamics. This is not so, for when private-for-profit firms are contracted, they receive from the government a guaranteed profit margin, and often additional "fees," all of which are paid for collectively by taxpayers. A firm contracting with the government does not receive its income from the individuals to whom it is providing the good or service; if individuals do pay any fees, they are not sufficient to cover the full cost of production and supply. Clients (now misleadingly called "customers") do not have a choice among competing providers. This is in no way a market (for details, see Chap. 4). This is pseudo-privatization, for the only thing that has been privatized is profit.

Governance. I use the term as traditionally and commonly defined: "the act, process, or power of governing; government" (Farlex 2011) or simply "activities originating with state institutions." I do <u>not</u> use the term to connote the idea of governance as "the multilateral cooperation of state institutions and non-state stakeholders" (Offe 2010, footnote 3).

State capture. The systematic creation of dependency of public authorities on private actors (Offe 2009).

Chapter 2
Case Examples: How Market Economics and Marketization Have Broken Government

The faith in market powers to fix what ails government is not only mistaken; in thousands of cases it is a central cause of "broken" government. In the United States, seeds of that blind faith were planted with the Reagan revolution and the introduction of "New Public Management" (NPM); they blossomed under a Clinton/Gore initiative called "Reinventing Government". Here are six examples:

Case examples (More details and an additional example are in Appendix A)	Market model (Assumption, principle or precept)
1. The real "waste of taxpayer money": contracting out	Efficiency/competition
2. Debtors' prisons return: "Offender-funded justice"	Revenue/profit maximization
3. Jobseekers denied help: the deviousness of "customer" choice	Virtue of individual choice
4. A free-market farce: procurement rules and the "Obamacare" website rollout	Efficiency/competition
5. Death by incentives: the V.A. performance bonus system	Rational utility maximization
6. Academic capitalism: "innovation" in higher education	Revenue/profit maximization

The Real "Waste of Taxpayer Money": Contracting-Out

Market Maxims: Efficiency and Competition

Contracting-out is a vast and growing part of the U.S. federal government. Contract spending mushroomed from $200 billion in 2000 to $530 billion in 2011. The total cost of federal contract employees is twice that of federal civil servants (Paul C.

© June A. Sekera 2016
J.A. Sekera, *The Public Economy in Crisis*,
SpringerBriefs in Economics, DOI 10.1007/978-3-319-40487-5_2

Light, as reported in Heires 2014). Indeed, the majority of government functions at the federal level may already have been outsourced, as several reports indicate that the ratio of private contract workers to civilian government employees may be four to one, or even much higher (Amey 2012a, b; DiIulio 2014; Verkuil 2007, p. 128; Light 2006).

Research has shown that contracting out is more expensive and less cost-efficient than direct government provision, which is contrary to beliefs shared by those inside and outside government (Sclar 2000), public workers and politicians, on the political left and right. This belief springs from the axiom of mainstream economics, itself unsupported, that markets are more efficient than government and that therefore private providers—inspired by the profit motive—are more efficient and will cost taxpayers less. The belief in the superiority of contracting out was, and remains, a central tenet of the "New Public Management" that dominates public administration today.

However, a thorough study by the Project on Government Oversight (POGO), shows contracting out to be far more expensive. Previous cost comparisons of public versus private provision have been marked by a common flaw: most have simply compared the compensation of government employees with that of private business employees in similar occupations, often found the former higher and concluded that contracting out is less expensive. Investigators had not thought, or bothered, to consider the full cost of contracted-out work—that is, contractors' actual billing rates, which include overhead costs and profit margins. The POGO study—*Bad Business* (Chassey and Amey 2011)—did just that, and found that "billions of dollars [are] wasted on hiring contractors" based on "a misguided assumption that market economies enable contractors to be more cost efficient than the government (Amey 2012). On average, contractors charged the federal government more than twice the amount it pays federal workers (Nixon 2011). There were, in fact and in effect, "*three labor markets* (the private sector, the public sector, and the contractor sector) and… salaries, compensation, overhead, and profit differ among the three" (Amey 2012). [Emphasis added.]

POGO's analysis (Chassey and Amey 2011, pp. 11–12) did not include any of the costs that government incurs to award, administer and oversee contracts or to have contractors work at federal facilities and use government equipment for free. Had they done so, contracting out would be revealed to be even more costly than POGO reported.

Debtors' Prisons Return: "Offender-Funded Justice"

Marketized Purpose: Revenue/Profit Generation as a Goal

Faced with declining tax revenues, counties and municipalities are turning over the operation of parts of the criminal justice system to private corporations that promise to provide legally mandated services at "no cost to taxpayers". These companies then charge fees to individuals accused of crimes or on probation to cover the costs of a legal system previously paid for collectively. Often already impoverished, those who can't pay the fees are now being imprisoned for debt.

In more than one thousand American courts it's not justice that is being served but local revenue generation and private profit. As one investigative report noted, the companies to whom states and localities have delegated such coercive power are subject to little oversight in their pursuit of maximum profits. For example, it's in the corporations' best interest to keep the collections process going, instead of calculating when probation has expired (Stillman 2014). "In many cases, the only reason people are put on probation is because they need time to pay off fines and court costs linked to minor crimes...[S]ervices that were once free, including those that are constitutionally required", are now frequently billed to offenders, [including] the cost of arrest warrants, DNA samples and a public defender..." (Edsall 2014; Shapiro 2014). "Technology, such as electronic monitors, aimed at helping defendants avoid jail time, is available only to those who can afford to pay for it" (Shapiro 2014). Companies have "a clear financial interest in extending probation terms in order to collect additional fees". And if defendants agree to wear electronic monitors in order to avoid jail time, those monitors themselves must be paid for; if they fall behind on this bill, they can be jailed (Choudhury 2014). Not even in 18th century debtors' prisons did prisoners have to pay for their manacles.[1]

Jobseekers Denied Help: The Deviousness of "Customer" Choice

Market Principle: The Virtue of Individual Choice

For thirty years the federally-funded employment and training system emphasized the value of case management by professional employment counselors helping the unemployed and underemployed prepare for and find jobs. Most of these jobseekers had never looked for full-time secure employment or hadn't looked in many years, so they needed help through the unfamiliar maze of "job searching", assessing job listings, writing resumes and preparing for interviews. Jobseekers were called "clients", an appellation of respect and an indication that people coming for job-seeking help merited professional guidance.

The Workforce Investment Act of 1998 revamped the entire system according to a set of market values that entailed "individual empowerment", "customer choice", and "self-service". Jobseekers were henceforth to be called "customers". "Customers" were directed to impersonal "resource rooms" where they had to conduct their own job searches at banks of computers, whether or not they had good

---

[1]The U.S. Department of Justice recently moved to curtail some of the abuses (Editorial Board, New York Times 2016).

computer skills. A few received "Individual Training Accounts"—another name for vouchers—that supposedly enabled them to choose an appropriate job-target and training. Local operators were to provide services "in a manner that *maximizes customer choice*" (Perez-Johnson and Decker 2001, p. 4). Counseling was minimized, case management often eliminated.

With little guidance, desperate jobseekers may take a low-paying job that has no long-term career prospects or become easy prey to unscrupulous, unsupervised private "training" providers who charge high fees and often deliver poor results. According to Carolyn Heinrich, professor of public affairs and economics at the University of Texas, Austin, "When job-seekers are eager for any career opportunity, unless those individuals have some independent reliable source of information, it's hard for them to make choices" (quoted in Chen 2014).

In an astute analysis of the consistently poor choices made by jobseekers given little guidance, Michele Chen (2014) points out that "The problem is an inherent asymmetry of information between the [training] companies and prospective students". Her own and other research reveals that "ultimately, people struggling to stay afloat might benefit from a structured job-training path, rather than individual "free choice"".

A 2014 extensive analysis of the Workforce Investment Act (Williams 2014) revealed that "many graduates wind up significantly worse off than when they started—mired in unemployment and debt from training for positions that do not exist, and [ending up] working elsewhere for minimum wage"—a predictable outcome when clients become customers.

"A Free-Market Farce": Procurement Rules and the "Obamacare" Website Rollout

Market Maxims: Efficiency and Competition

Behind the disastrous rollout of the "Obamacare" website in October 2013 is a story of government attempts at market mimicry going back several decades. It is a story about government procurement—a boring topic, you may think. But changes to federal procurement rules[2]—designed in the 1990s to incorporate the alleged virtues of streamlined market competition—have had daily impacts on millions of lives.

As explained by Janine Wedel and Linda Keenan (2010, quoted in detail in the Appendix), the procurement rules were revamped in ways that persistently benefit

---

[2]In a forerunner to the 1990s changes, market "solutions" as procurement policy goes back to the Reagan era with its implementation of the "A-76" procurement doctrine, which itself goes back to the Eisenhower era.

bidders while compromising the public interest. Wedel and Keenan call the revamped rules "a free market farce". Still operative, the rules went unquestioned when the Obama administration decided to contract out to a for-profit corporation the development of the website for the Affordable Care Act.

Due to the bidder advantages conferred by these rules, the Obama administration chose as the principal contractor a firm with a documented history of incompetence in prior government work. The website crashed upon rollout, giving the Obama administration an enormous black eye and deepening an already wide-spread belief in government incompetence. But the debacle of the ACA website rollout cannot be laid at the door of simple government incompetence, except insofar as those in charge at the top failed to appreciate the predictable pitfalls of a procurement process designed according to market maxims, and effectively oriented in favor of profit-seeking bidders.

Death by Incentives: The V.A. Performance Bonus System

Market Principles: Rational Choice; Utility Maximization

Public performance measurement systems often have unfortunate or disastrous unintended consequences. In the United States, a pay-for-performance scheme at the Veterans Health Administration (V.A.) led to falsified wait-time records and care so delayed that, in some cases, patients allegedly died awaiting medical attention.

Twenty-five years of studies have shown that "pay-for-performance" doesn't work in either the public or private sector: such systems smother creativity, crowd out intrinsic motivation, invite gaming and generally fail to achieve intended results (Economist 2014c; Frey and Osterloh 2012; Lagace 2003; Carroll 2014). Yet market advocates within government have imposed federal pay-for-performance systems, with the Clinton administration introducing performance–driven metrics throughout the V.A. in the 1990s (Markkula Center 2014) and the Bush administration successfully pushing V.A. performance bonus legislation that was implemented in 2006 (Committee on Veterans Affairs, US Senate, 2004). Ultimately, the V.A. tied senior staff bonus payments to meeting a 14-day patient appointment wait-time target—a higher standard than set or met in private healthcare.

Fast forward to 2014 and the scandal in which V.A. employees—faced with low morale and staff vacancies, burgeoning patient loads and supervisors whose pay depended in part on showing how short wait-times had been achieved—falsified reports about the ever-longer time that sick veterans had to wait for appointments.

The gaming of ill-designed systems is familiar in the private as well as public sector, but faith in market medicine blinded both Republican and Democratic administrations to this predictable, "rationally perverse" response (Moynihan and Soss 2014, pp. 328–329) to pressures created by such systems. In the aftermath of the scandal, the performance bonus system was temporarily suspended. But the system was reaffirmed in "reform" legislation passed in August 2014 (Tritten 2014). And in line with calls for greater marketization and privatization (Cappiello 2014; *Wall Street Journal* 2014), the legislation also privatized some aspects of V.A. medical care.

Academic Capitalism: "Innovation" in Higher Education

Market Maxims: Revenue/Profit Maximization

In recent years, the idea of higher education as a public good has been losing out to the notion that public universities should adopt market-based principles and practices, with income production as their goal.

"Academic capitalism", as it has been called since the work of Slaughter and Leslie (1997), is a growing phenomenon, linked by Slaughter and Rhoades (2004) to the "corporatization of education", which has taken us from a public goods paradigm to an "academic capitalism knowledge regime [that] values knowledge privatization and profit taking in which institutions, inventor faculty, and corporations have claims that come before those of the public" (Talburt 2005).

For several decades now, British universities have been undergoing aspects of marketization. Marina Warner (2015) has vividly described the "denaturing of the universities" in the UK through a "Research Excellence Framework" (REF) that "pushes responsibility from persons to systems. It pushes individuals to one side and replaces them with columns, boxes, numbers, rubrics, [and] often meaningless tautologies…" The REF calls "the work of writing a book 'generating an output' or a university 'a knowledge delivery solution'…[and sets writing and research] in the mold of market ideology, as sales items".

Recent developments in the American political arena suggest that the push toward academic capitalism is accelerating here. Writing in the *Washington Post* after the 2014 elections, two conservative columnists (Ponnuru and Levin 2014) opined that "our higher education system desperately needs market discipline", and they support "Republican reformers interested in enhancing the market orientation of the higher education sector…".

Economics and Economists

My argument is that mainstream, market-centric economics has been broadly and dangerously transformative within government and public institutions. Market-centric economics is the smog that pervades the atmosphere of public policy and public administration, a smog that has at once caused and obscured each of the failures described above. "Economic abstraction has been coupled with power to impose that abstraction throughout [the nation]. The result has been a political economy that generates the conditions for its own failure…".[3]

Of course, economic precepts must be transmitted and applied by people—by economists. Economists have enormous influence in our country, as elsewhere (Fourcade et al. 2014). As Paul Samuelson once said (Weinstein 2009), "I don't care who writes a nation's laws…if I can write its economics textbooks".

Some economists, like Victoria Chick of University College London (Chick 2011, 2013), have been advocating an overhaul of the pedagogy of economics to reverse much of the damage done by a market-driven system of values—a system that has colonized "much of academic inquiry in the social sciences" and "public debate as a whole". We should no longer acquiesce to the unsubstantiated axioms of mainstream economics that have lent pseudo-scientific support "to programmes of deregulation and privatization over the past 40 years".

As it stands now, students in university economics courses inevitably learn about the superiority of markets from a professoriate that transmits the reigning market-centric economics, that speaks regularly of government as little more than an impediment to "efficient markets" and that understands public goods as "a problem" of "market failure". In the United States, about 40 % of college students take at least one economics course (Goodwin 2014a); after graduation more than half of economics majors go to work in government (Kalambokidis 2014). So each of the federal agencies involved in the sad cases above is populated by economists who themselves have been taught to distrust government and to look to the market for best practices.

---

[3]Bowman et al. (2014). The authors write principally about the UK, but their argument brilliantly captures the American reality too.

Chapter 3
A Failed Private-to-Public Transplant: "New Public Management"

Public administration as practiced in the United States today is hostage to market-centric economics. "New Public Management" (NPM) is the name given by public administration scholars[1] to the privatization and marketization movement that commands center stage. An extensive academic literature tracks NPM from its start in the U.S. under Reagan and in the U.K. under Thatcher, its spread to Australia and New Zealand in the late 1980s and 1990s, and to more than sixty countries since (Rosta 2011).

NPM did not emerge from public administration theory; rather, it is a real-world manifestation of neoclassical economic theory. "New Public Management" is merely a label that public administration scholars have given to a phenomenon that has happened within the real world public sector over the last three to four decades. It is practice that came out of a creed, and it has been imposed by both progressive and conservative politicians and public leaders, who rely on the alleged superiority of the market model as their rationale. As practiced across the US today by those who lead, control or manage in government (with a few exceptions), public administration adheres to a nearly-universal, and mainly uncritical, acceptance of the paradigm of market superiority. Rank and file workers in government agencies have increasingly bought into the mantra that government should be "run like a business" and have endeavored to implement the market-mimicking practices that they have been instructed to embrace and make work.[2]

---

[1]The term "New Public Management" was coined by Christopher Hood in 1991 according to Christensen and Laegreid (2011, p. 1).

[2]Not all public workers have meekly accepted the imposition of market values and practices. Some, especially in Europe, have protested and resisted; others have been deeply conflicted. See, among others, Siltala (2013), Dahl and Soss (2012).

© June A. Sekera 2016
J.A. Sekera, *The Public Economy in Crisis*,
SpringerBriefs in Economics, DOI 10.1007/978-3-319-40487-5_3

What Is the "New Public Management"?

"You cannot see, touch, smell or hear the NPM," writes Christopher Pollitt, a widely-cited scholar of New Public Management, which he describes (Pollitt 2007, p. 10) as "a rhetorical and conceptual construction and, like all such constructions, … open to re-interpretation and shifting usages over time." Less hesitant to define its essence, Stephen Osborne, Professor of International Public Management, University of Edinburgh, has called NPM "a child of neoclassical economics and particularly rational/public choice theory" (Osborne 2006).

While elements of marketization began to appear in the U.S. government under the Carter administration, the creed of market superiority, in tandem with the belief that government was "the problem, not the solution," lay at the heart of the agenda of the succeeding Reagan administration, which established the foundation for NPM through a host of new administrative rules and procedures.[3] Subsequently, broad-based market-centric values and norms, as well as additional specific practices, were instilled and installed by the Clinton/Gore administration through its "National Performance Review" initiative, otherwise known as "Reinventing Government." Intended ostensibly to improve operations, the fundamental effect of the initiative was to entrench (allegedly) market-like practices within government.

Despite three decades of work in, and consulting for, governments at all levels and across the country, I never once heard the term "New Public Management" in the halls of government. I encountered it only when I began to read the academic literature on public administration. In practice, what I and my colleagues experienced on the ground was no philosophical treatise on governance but the pro-market prescriptions of the Clinton/Gore administration. Those of us working in Massachusetts had previously experienced such prescriptions as promulgated by David Osborne, who had been appointed by Governor Weld to the Massachusetts Jobs Council that oversaw the programs of the state agency that ran public jobs programs. In 1992, Osborne and Ted Gaebler wrote *Reinventing Government: How the Entrepreneurial Spirit Is Transforming the Public Sector*, (Osborne, D. and Gaebler 1992) the book that kicked off the movement across the U.S. and gave it its

---

[3]Such as the "A-76" administrative rules that imposed a regimen for contracting-out.

name. Osborne later became active in the National Academy of Public Administration, which further advanced the movement.

For readers unfamiliar with the New Public Management literature, here is a sampling of representative descriptions by public administration scholars:

Thomas Diefenbach (2009), in his summary of the NPM literature, noted both NPM's aggressive expansiveness and its market-centrism. "The movement is both radical and total in its scope as well as in its intensity, as the following list demonstrates

- It has been introduced to all public service sectors ...
- It is an increasingly global phenomenon ...
- In Anglo-Saxon and European countries at least, it has been supported by all major political parties, for example, by Republicans and Democrats, and by Conservatives and Labour governments."

From the *Ashgate Research Companion to New Public Management* (Christensen and Laegreid 2011, p. xvi) we have:

NPM is a shopping basket of different instruments, measures and tools including both market-and management-related features. Some of the main components of NPM [include] structural devolution, autonomy and agencification; performance management, auditing and ex post control; managerialism and management models; marketization, competition and privatization; and public-private partnerships.

Siegrun Fox Freyss (2014) captured NPM's essentials and succinctly described its U.S. origins.

The competitive, market-driven public administration model can be summarized in terms of three developments promoted in theory and practice:

- The privatization of government functions, also called load-shedding,
- Contracting for services from other jurisdictions and from for-profit or nonprofit enterprises,
- The adoption of management tools developed by the private sector.

The privatization movement had its heydays in the eighties, promoted by President Reagan with his New Federalism policies, as well as by like-minded authors. For a time, there was strong opposition to this policy, especially among unionized workers and advocates of the poor. However, the opposition slowly declined.

Siegrun Fox Freyss continues:

David Osborne and Ted Gaebler can be credited for making the approaches acceptable to public managers with their book *Reinventing Government: How the Entrepreneurial Spirit Is Transforming the Public Sector*, published in 1992. The book was written in a positive, can-do tone that Democrats could embrace, including the Clinton administration. The model lives on in the public administration literature as New Public Management, which is an unfortunate descriptor since a 30-year old policy direction can hardly be called "new."

"New Public Management—The Evidence-Based Worst Practice?"

In a paper whose title, above, is a dig at popular practices in public administration today, the historian Juha Siltala (2013) describes how NPM has "fitted public services into quasimarket models"—with the result that, in important ways, "Western societies are sliding toward the failed states of Third World..." In his critical assessment of the impacts of NPM, Siltala finds that NPM,

> introduced punishments and rewards to produce better services with lesser staff. Instead of having freed energies and creativity of employees formerly shackled by their bureaucratic turfs, NPM reforms have bound energies into theatrical audit performances at the cost of work and killed creativity in centralizing resources and hollowing out professional autonomy... Fundamental deprivation of the legitimacy of public employees. . .has traumatized many most-committed employees and driven others toward a Soviet-type double standard.

Notwithstanding the voluminous literature on NPM, we have little hard evidence of NPM delivering on any of its promises. Christopher Pollitt et al. (2013) after compiling a database of 518 studies of NPM in Europe, determined that "more than 90 % of what are seen by experts as the most significant and relevant studies contain no data at all on outcomes" and that of the 10 % that had outcomes information, only 44 % of those, or 4 % of the total, found any improvements in terms of outcomes. Pollitt adds:

> The claim is NOT that many of the organizations in many of these studies are naked of performance information – on the contrary, they often have rather a lot of it...[but] they hardly ever have solid information about the final outcomes or impacts of management reforms on their clients or on the wider society (p 4).

Thomas Diefenbach (2009), who has also examined NPM in Europe, summarizes the analyses of scholars who found negative consequences of NPM strategies on public sector organizations and the people working in them. He concludes that, "At present we are witnessing the devaluation, if not to say destruction, of public goods and services as well as of the public service ethos at a global scale."

On this side of the Atlantic, reliable assessments of the implementation of NPM are even harder to find. One trenchant analysis of the Clinton administration's National Performance Review was published by Ronald Moe (1994), a year after the initiative was announced with "high expectations and considerable fanfare" by Vice President Gore. The occasion followed the 1993 release of the "Gore Report," entitled *From Red Tape to Results: Creating a Government That Works Better and Costs Less,* which was largely written by David Osborne and echoed the maxims of the Osborne-Gabler book on government reinvention.[4] In Moe's analysis the Gore

---

[4]Besides Moe's summary of Osborne's involvement, David Osborne's online bio at the Reason Foundation states that he was the "chief author of the NPR report, which laid out the Clinton Administration's reinvention agenda".

Report and its sequels constituted a "major attack" on the "administrative management paradigm" that derives from the constitutional foundation of governance, which

> accepted as its fundamental premise that the government of the United States is a government of laws passed by the representatives of the people assembled in Congress. It is the constitutional responsibility of the President and his duly appointed and approved subordinates to see that these laws, wise and unwise, are implemented.

The Gore Report insisted on a different paradigm, entrepreneurial management, as Moe explains:

> [T]he report is seeking to break the public law basis of an agency's mission and replace it with an "outcomes" mission orientation as defined by the agency's political chief. [But] The management of the executive branch is not like the management of General Electric or the Ritz-Carlton Hotels [cited as model by the Report]. The mission of government agencies is determined by the representatives of the people, not agency management.

So Moe predicted that:

> The net result of the Gore Report when its recommendations are implemented to the maximum degree possible in the political realm will be a government much less accountable to the citizens for its performance. Contractors and consultants will enjoy even greater management responsibilities for government programs... [emphasis added].

In an essay on the "Myth of the Bureaucratic Paradigm," public administration scholar Laurence E. Lynn, Jr. (2001) shared Moe's concern about the ways in which revisionist new public management movements detach public administration from its traditional grounding in law and the Constitution. Lynn concluded (p. 155):

> Often missing in literature and discourse is recognition that reformers of institutions and civic philosophies must show how the capacity to effect public purposes and accountability to the polity will be enhanced in a manner that comports with our Constitution and our republican institutions. Basic political and legal issues of responsible management in a postmodern era are inadequately defined and addressed. Such a result ill becomes a profession that once owned impressively deep insight into public administration in a representative democracy. [Emphasis added].

When Gaebler responded to some of the academic attacks upon NPM (Gaebler and Miller 2006), he inadvertently confirmed suspicions about the roots of the ideas for Reinventing Government (and the embrace of market models), admitting (p. 21) that "Reinvention is an updated version of Tiebout's public choice model, which has influenced the study of public economics for over 50 years."

Government reinvention was more than a rallying cry. The message of an administrative "revolution" (the word the White House used in a 1993 press release) (White House Office of Domestic Policy) was maintained throughout the Clinton administration, and perpetuated in Vice President Gore's 1997 manual on businesslike government. A survey of public administration scholars by David Kasdan (2012) found that the "most influential" public administration book of the previous twenty years had been *Reinventing Government*, though "almost universally derided" by Kasdan's academic respondents.

Many observers and scholars have called attention to the sweeping change that has been wrought. "NPM is a new paradigm"—said Neil Collins (2012) in "Challenging New Public Management." In their book on managing a contracted-out government, David Frederickson and George Frederickson (2006, p. 10) say that "The performance measurement movement [that has grown out of the NPM movement] has influenced all modern governments and could fairly be described as a fundamental reform in public administration."

Language has power. As Moe notes (1994, p. 113), the reinventing government initiative "largely rejects the traditional language of administrative discourse which attempts, not always with success, to employ terms with precise meanings. Instead, a new highly value-laden lexicon is employed by entrepreneurial management enthusiasts to disarm would-be questioners. Thus, the term 'customer' largely replaces 'citizen' and there is heavy reliance upon active verbs—reinventing, reengineering, empowering—to maximize the emotive content of what otherwise has been a largely nonemotive subject matter."

Perhaps if instead of naming the phenomenon "New Public Management," theorists had named it "Old Market Management," they would be on a different course than they are today. In any event, the concept that took root within U.S. government, and that is still the reigning orthodoxy, is that of the superiority of the market. Public administration theorists have observed and commented on the phenomenon and given it a name, but rather than spending time studying its outcomes empirically and rigorously (in the US at least), they have turned to the development of new, substitute theories. Yet, though the essence of New Public Management, aka Reinventing Government, arises from the market-centric arena of economic theory, all *would-be replacements for NPM ignore or skirt economics.*

Would-Be Replacements for NPM: Recent Public Administration Theory

Largely in reaction to NPM, new theories of public administration have been advanced by public administration scholars. The main theoretical contenders attempting to replace NPM seem to be the following:

- New Public Service
- Public Value theory
- New Public Governance

These governance theories are discussed in more detail in Appendix B.

None has noticeably taken root and most have not been put into actual government practice in the United States, where market values continue to reign across the public sector.[5]

None of the advocates of these new theories proposes how to deal with the central issue of neoclassical economics as the intellectual source of the market-centricity of current practice, and the resultant destruction of government's operating capabilities. Most focus instead on civic engagement and citizen participation in the co-production of public goods and services. This approach slights the centrality of electorally-manifested collective choice as the foundation of governance in a democratic nation-state. Focusing on idealized citizen engagement leaves in place the marketized, depleted, hollowed-out core of public governance. The new theorists do not explain how such a depleted public workforce can hope to add citizen engagement to a growing set of responsibilities for public production in the face of resources that are being slashed, and slashed again.

Finally, the theorists fail to address the malign effects of the fact that much of public service delivery has already been contracted out to private corporations. Indeed, public administration theory in general does not take into consideration the extent to which the privatization of government has depleted it of talent, know-how and institutional memory. An exception is a book on "third-party government" and the "hollowed-out state" by Frederickson and Frederickson (2006), who detail the ways in which contracting out has disabled government. But this dismantling of core government capacity is not effectively addressed by the would-be replacements for New Public Management.

Conclusion

The question for all of the new governance theorists is exactly this: How to restore the role of the state as a strategic agent that creates and implements collectively binding solutions on behalf of all citizens.

This restoration cannot be achieved so long as theorists of public administration overlook the distinctive nature of government as a non-market producer of goods

---

[5]Beryl Radin, public administration scholar and former practitioner, tells us (2012, p. 18): "From the Progressive Era onward, efficiency values and the concept of a market have been the predominant values for public administration." Furthermore (p. 36), "It is important to recognize that the borrowing process seems to work in just one direction; I am not aware of any instances in which the private sector borrowed techniques from the public sector. The private sector appears to be happy if the relationship is limited to the financial transfer of public funds to private sources".

and services. Neither public administration scholars nor economists are drawing out clear, actionable connections between neoclassical economic theory and the public administration issues that are at the root of the "broken government" we have today.

In a speech at the Woodrow Wilson School of Government, Paul Volcker (2014) relayed an anecdote about an economics professor at Princeton who once had told him that "public administration [is] not an appropriate matter for a great university; public administration is not an intellectual discipline like economics." Volcker might have replied: Is it not one of the foremost intellectual challenges of our times to figure out a rational, useful and effective way for a democratic society to jointly produce the goods and services it collectively needs for its continued well-being? And he might have asked: Why has economics shrunk from this challenge?

Chapter 4
Why the Transplant Doesn't Work

We lack an economic theory of the public non-market economy. Profiting from this void, market advocates have imposed the assumptions and axioms of neoclassical economics wholesale on the public sector. There are severe, tangible consequences to this colonization, which has drastically undermined government's ability to produce desired and intended results.

In the first part of this chapter, I present a series of arguments about why particular assumptions and precepts of the market model do not and cannot work when transplanted onto the public nonmarket.

These will be my rubrics:

Market mimicry: faux competition in a pseudo-market

- No buyers, no sellers, no exchange
- The powerless monopsonist
- Crowding-in
- The results-consequences disconnect
- The contractor sector
- The mythology of choice
- The real "principal-agent problem": fundamentally conflicting purposes
- The mythology of shrinking government
- Invisibility as a hallmark of effectiveness
- The (near) inability to measure what matters.

In the second part, I hone in on some of the particularly destructive effects of market mimicry:

- De-democratization
- A perversion of purpose: revenue-raising becomes a goal
- The conversion of citizens into "customers"
- The hollowing-out of government

© June A. Sekera 2016
J.A. Sekera, *The Public Economy in Crisis*,
SpringerBriefs in Economics, DOI 10.1007/978-3-319-40487-5_4

- Disregard for the biophysical aspects of production
- The frustrated quest for efficiency
- Performance measurement practices produce unintended and injurious results.

Market Assumptions and Precepts that Don't Fit a Nonmarket

Transplanting market theory and precepts onto the real-world operations of the public non-market yields results that are frequently and predictably destructive, sometimes disastrous. In previous chapters, I reviewed several such examples. In this chapter I will draw tighter connections between some of the fundamental assumptions and assertions of mainstream economics and the types of problems that inevitably arise when they are applied to the public non-market—problems that deeply affect people's lives.

My intent here is not to rehearse the multitude of challenges to neoclassical economics that have been and are being mounted by pluralist economists. Rather, I mean to identify those precepts and assumptions that are most troubling when transplanted to the public non-market. Identifying these defective connections will help reveal conceptual threads that can be woven into a new tapestry—a rich and realistic model of the public non-market economy.

My other intent is to draw new connections between economics and public administration. Just as there are many critics of neoclassical economics, there are likewise many critics, and criticisms, of the New Public Management, the Reinventing Government movement, and moves toward privatization. But for decades the two fields—economics and public administration—have been divorced.[1] The critical analyses of economics and of public administration take place now in different worlds. I hope to bring those two worlds closer together by examining the degradation of government capabilities through the lens of economics.

A final point to make before offering my analysis is that, although not everyone may endorse (or even be acquainted with), the theories of mainstream economics, its axioms are deeply ingrained in our society. Consider, for example, the market-centric notion of competitiveness, which has become, as William Davies (2014b) tells us, "one of the great unquestioned virtues of contemporary culture. . . a supreme moral and cultural virtue." Given how ingrained this and other market-centric values have become in our culture, it is not surprising that within government there is a prevailing acceptance of market and business superiority. I have discussed how the seeds for this credulity within government were planted

---

[1]"Public choice" theory, of course, purportedly explains government from an economics perspective. However, as I will argue in Chap. 6, it rests on manifestly anti-government axioms and market-centric assertions rather than offering a coherent, explanatory economic analysis.

over three decades ago. The belief system, and accompanying norms of behavior, are now firmly implanted. James Galbraith (2008, p. xvii) talks about the "Soviet-like" double reality that exists in regard to "the cult of the free market": the governing "legitimating" myth [is] hardly to be taken seriously by those on the inside", i.e., those who propagate it. However, many—probably the majority—in government have bought into the myth. But it's not enough to understand that those on the "inside" know better. We must develop an alternative to the myth, a legitimate, pragmatic "idea infrastructure" (Mcgarity 2013a, b) that can supplant myths with valid concepts. I will offer such an alternative in Chap. 5.

Market Mimicry: Faux Competition in a Pseudo-Market

The entrenched government reform agenda in the U.S., and in many European countries, has been based on the assertion that there is a need for more market- and market-like mechanisms in government. The fundamental idea, as Kettl says (1993, p. 2), is to "replace the government's monopoly with the discipline of vigorous competition." He labels it "the competition prescription".

There have been two kinds of reformers, Kettl says, those who want to shrink government[2] and those who want to make government work better. But in either case, reformers have offered the same prescription: marketize government, either by contracting out its work or by transplanting market (business) values and practices onto what's left.[3]

When a government activity is marketized or privatized, it is widely believed that "market mechanisms" have been introduced into government because a ritual resembling "competition" has been undertaken.[4] But there is not competition. There is merely faux competition in a pseudo-market. Competition—as the term is generally understood, and as used in economics—is impossible in the production of public products (i.e., taxpayer-funded goods and services, as I will discuss in Chap. 5).

I should note that although the term "privatization" is not used in economics, as a popularized stand-in for the values and precepts of mainstream economics it is highly relevant to my analysis. "Privatization" as used in the United States, is

---

[2]It has been pointed out that many of the "shrink government" reformers do not aim actually to reduce the size of government, but rather to transform its operations into profit-making, private wealth-generating arrangements for corporations. Contracted-out government is, in fact, the source of the much-remarked "growth of government".

[3]Recently, several new public administration theories have emerged, which attempt to offer alternative prescriptions, but, as I discussed earlier, these movements have neither engaged with the fundamental problem of a flawed economic model, nor have they become practice except in limited instances.

[4]Even Kettl, who questions the whole approach, believes (1993, p. vii) that genuine market mechanisms are introduced.

understood to mean contracting out government services to private businesses. Virtually every source I found in my research, and certainly the popular media, accepts the trope that "privatizing" government introduces competition and the advantages of the market. It is a virtually unquestioned assumption. But the assumption is false.

The term "privatization" is duplicitous, in that the putative virtues of the market, such as efficiency and cost-effectiveness, are infrequently realized by contracting out to private firms. In fact, contracting out often results in higher costs and inefficiencies (as I describe later). Virtually no one points out the deceptiveness. One exception is Juha Siltala, who has coined phrases that emphasize the rampant duplicity. In his essay on "New Public Management: The Evidence-Based Worst Practice?" (2013, pp. 469, 472, 473, 475, 477), Siltala probes "quasimarkets," "proxy markets" and "pseudoprivatization."

Now back to the pseudo-market and faux competition.

In standard microeconomics, a competitive market assumes the following conditions (Goodwin et al. 2014; Kettle 1993):

1. a large number of buyers and sellers;
2. relatively undifferentiated goods and services, so that buyers make decisions based on price;
3. free entry and exit;
4. arms-length transactions between sellers and buyers;
5. buyers and sellers with perfect information;
6. reward for success and punishment for failure.[5]

None of these applies to the public nonmarket, where

- Government is the single purchaser, i.e., a monopsonist (albeit a powerless one, as explained later);
- As buyer, government decisions are made on a number of considerations of which price is but one. Also, the executive branch is frequently (as in the case of defense contracting) required by legislation to contract on a fixed-cost-plus-fee basis, in which case the government is denied the ability to purchase at lowest cost.
- Government agencies (the producers) cannot choose either to create themselves or to go out of business.
- Purchasing transactions between the government and its suppliers are often not at arms-length; they are characterized more usually by mutual dependence (Kettl 1993, pp. 12, 182–83)
- Government actors generally lack information about which price is lowest.[6]

---

[5]An interpretation stressed by Kettl (1993, p. 180).

[6]This problem is also present in the market, but much moreso in the public nonmarket. Regarding government's inability to determine best price, see the Project on Government Operation's report "Bad Business" (Chassey and Amey 2011).

- Because of the uncommon complexity, difficulty and sometimes impossibility of measuring results, income to the producer (government agency) is not based on measures of success or failure.

Nor are the following *implicit assumptions* about competitive markets applicable:

- Buyers are using their own money,
- Sellers can decide what to produce and sell,
- Goods and services are paid for by the person or entity receiving them,
- Buyers are able to "see" what they are paying for,

  for in the public nonmarket

- payment is made collectively by taxpayers;
- legislators decide the uses to which collectively-raised money will be put, i.e., what government will produce;
- a third party—a body of elected representatives—is the direct payer;
- taxpayers may not be able to see, or recognize, much of what their taxes buy.

I will elaborate on each of these points in the remainder of this chapter, and in Chap. 5, where I discuss elements of public non-market production."

No Buyers, No Sellers, No Exchange

In the public products economy, goods and services are supplied free at the point of delivery. (When there are fees, these are not meant to cover the entire cost of production and supply.) In contrast to the market model, there are no buyers or sellers; there is no "exchange."

In the market model, individuals buy goods and services to maximize their own utility (or satisfaction). The buyer is the beneficiary. Buyers pay using their own money; if they have borrowed, they must repay with their own money. By contrast, in the public non-market economy, there are no "buyers" in the usual sense of that term: goods and services have been paid for collectively, through taxes.

Rather than "buyers," the public non-market has a "purchasing agent" (the government agency doing the buying). This agent is not the beneficiary and is not using its own money. The Purchasing Agent uses taxpayer money; the beneficiary is the recipient or user of the publicly provided good or service.

The Powerless Monopsonist

In economics, monopsony exists when there is a market with a single buyer. Microeconomic theory tells us that a monopsonist can dictate terms to its suppliers and drive prices down. However, government as a monopsonist buyer is often rendered powerless by private interests acting through political force or by the ambient pressure to contract out. Three examples:

- When Medicare Part D legislation was being considered, the drug lobby succeeded in prohibiting the government from being able to negotiate drug prices (Pierce 2009). "The drug lobby worked hard to ensure Medicare wouldn't be allowed to cut into the profits which would flow to big Pharma thanks to millions of new customers delivered to them by Part D." The prices that the government pays for drugs through Part D are 30 % higher on average than the prices it pays for drugs for recipients of Medicaid, which is not constrained by a prohibition against negotiating prices.
- Due to a convoluted procurement process, which at one point involved a private contractor managing part of the procurement process, the government wound up paying higher rates for a phone system than federal agencies could have gotten if they had been allowed to pay commercially-available rates (Kettl 1993, pp. 77, 94–95).
- "Medicare's authorizing legislation…requires it to contract on a cost basis, prohibiting CMS from entering into fixed-price or performance-based contracts" (Frederickson and Frederickson 2006, p. 178).

Crowding-in

One of the axioms of mainstream economics is that government spending "crowds out" private spending, causing economic inefficiencies. This long-held assertion has recently been disproven. A study by the International Monetary Fund (Economist 2014b) found "that in rich countries at least, infrastructure spending can significantly boost growth through higher demand in the short run and through higher supply in the long run." The results of the study, writes *The Economist*, "were striking. On average, an unexpected increase in public investment equal to 1 % of GDP boosted GDP by an underwhelming but still beneficial 0.4 % in the same year and by a more impressive 1.5 % four years later. The extra spending did not result in unsustainable debts; quite the opposite. Thanks to higher GDP, the debt-to-GDP ratio fell by 0.9 % points in the first year and four percentage points after four years." A World Bank study of low-income countries (Eden and Kray 2014) also disproved the "crowding-out" claim; in fact, the researchers found strong evidence of crowding in: "an extra dollar of government investment raises private investment by roughly two dollars, and output by 1.5 dollars." So we have here another case in which traditional neoclassical economic theory is inapplicable, or wrong, and should be put aside.

The Results-Consequences Disconnect

As Donald Kettl points out (1993, p. 180): "The much-praised self-discipline [efficiency] of the market exists only when competition can reward success and punish failure."

Success or failure in the market is measured in simple, financial terms. Profitability means continued survival; loss of profits results, eventually, in business demise. Money is both the fuel for production and the gauge by which success, or failure, is determined.

The public non-market is not blessed with such simplicity. In the domain of the public nonmarket, money is also the fuel for production, but it is not—or should not be—the gauge of success. As I argue in Chap. 5, the driver in the public domain is not profit-maximization; rather, it is the meeting of identified public needs, expressed through electoral collective choice. So success must be gauged by the extent to which the identified need was met. Such measurement is uncommonly difficult—a theme I develop later when I discuss the elements of nonmarket production. For now, the point is that, since we lack effective measures of success or failure, one of the conceptual foundations of the market model is missing. So a producer of clean air (Environmental Protection Agency), a producer of warnings of potentially disastrous weather conditions (National Weather Service), or a producer of healthful recreation (state parks) have all faced funding cuts regardless of their success. Conversely, public economic development subsidies to businesses continue, despite their widely-documented lack of success in achieving their stated goals.[7] In sum, there is a results-consequences disconnect in the public non-market that does not exist in the market.

A vast performance measurement/performance management industry has been attempting to make results measurable in the public sector, such that good results should be rewarded and poor results punished (Christensen and Laegreid 2011). Thus far this goal has not been achieved—a point to which I shall return.

The Contractor Sector

Some researchers who have studied government contracting believe that a generally unrecognized or under-appreciated third sector exists—neither public nor private but rather a "contractor sector". For example, the Project on Government Oversight (POGO), conducting an extensive study of federal contracting in 2011, came to the realization that "there are three labor markets (the private sector, the public sector, and the contractor sector) and that salaries, compensation, overhead, and profit

---

[7]Good Jobs First has extensively documented the failures of economic development programs to create jobs. See Story (2012a–c) for a *New York Times* series on "The United States of Subsidies."

differ among the three." The POGO study (Amey 2012a) showed that "the federal government approves service contract billing rates—deemed fair and reasonable—that pay contractors 1.83 times more than the government pays federal employees in total compensation, and more than 2 times the total compensation paid in the private sector for comparable services." In his book on government contracting, Kettl (1993, pp. 94–95) cited one case in which federal agencies were paying 20 % higher rates than those commercially available. Here we have another example—the contractor sector—in which "competition" does not exist or work as the market model predicts.

The Mythology of Choice

Most mainstream economists (and some public administration scholars[8]) argue that taxes force involuntary choice while markets don't. This is a myth. Both the market and the public non-market require payment and both permit choice of what to pay for.

In the market, there is choice about *what* to buy and *how much* to pay for it. There is no choice about *whether* to pay for it. Payment is required.

So too in the public non-market: *whether* to pay is not voluntary. Paying taxes is required. And, as in the market, *what* to pay for and *how much* of it is voluntary. Society can have more or less public transit, greater or less assurance of drug safety, more or fewer public parks or safe bicycle lanes in the city, and so forth. In this case, the choices are made at the ballot box. Through their choice of elected representatives, voters determine the type and quantity of public goods and services that will be created. That the choice is delegated does not negate the fact that there is choice. It is time to expose and rebut the myth that there is no choice in the public sector and only in the market.

The Real Principal-Agent Problem: Fundamentally Conflicting Purposes

Principal-agent theory in neoclassical economics addresses differing motivations between principals and agents, as between supervisors and employees or firms and contractors. Theoretical discussions deal with issues like "shirking" by agents. But principal-agent theory does not address the highly significant if generally unremarked problem that occurs when a public principal (government) contracts with a private-for-profit agent (a business) to deliver public goods or services. In this

---

[8]James Q. Wilson (1989) goes so far as to write that "public enterprise is funded with money taken from us by force" (p. 348).

situation the mission of the agent (to make a profit) is in conflict with the raison d'être of the principal (to meet a public need, not to generate revenue).

And the problem of fundamental conflict goes deeper than merely identifying profit as a goal. Two fundamentals of profit-generation that are often overlooked in discussions about contracting-out, and in principal-agent theory, are contractors' needs for growth and for repeat business. Growth is the preferred, and sometimes the only, method for increasing profits. The conflict in fundamental purpose is particularly problematic, and can be morally repugnant, when the public "product" being "delivered" is public safety. The most egregious example may be the ongoing privatization of prisons and of the probation system, where the avenue to increased profits is more prisoners and more probationers, and where private-for-profit "corrections" corporations draft and campaign to ensure the passage of laws to increase the number of prisoners and/or the prescribed length of prison terms (Center for Media and Democracy 2015b).

The second way the conflict manifests itself is through efforts to get repeat business so as to sustain profitability. Contractors work to ensure that they get future contracts from their federal "principals." In *Sharing Power*, Kettl (1993) wrote at length about the relationship of "mutual dependency" that grows between federal contractors and the government. Contractors go to great lengths to guarantee continued demand from their single buyer.

In textbook principal-agent theory, the "problem" is normally discussed in antiseptic, morally-neutral terms. But what occurs in public-private principal-agent relationships can be a perversion of purpose. The operations of the public agency can be transformed from meeting a public need to, instead, work that is designed to exploit opportunities for growth or guarantee repeat business.

In the market, sustained profit-generation is the legitimate purpose of business, embodied in law and accepted almost universally in our society. My point is not to criticize these behaviors in the market, but to point to a fundamental conflict that is generally overlooked.

Consider a remarkable example of how the issue is overlooked. In his textbook on *Economics of the Public Sector* Joseph Stiglitz (2000, pp. 202–03) describes the principal-agent problem as one in which citizens (principals) must get public servants (agents) to act in the public interest. Stiglitz has chosen to rely on the Public Choice school of economics, with its claim that self-interest is the motivator of public employees, a basic assumption of the market model. So this major text on the public economy is oblivious to the real-world conflict of purpose that I describe here.

The Mythology of Shrinking Government

One of the maxims of privatizers is that if government operations are contracted out to marketplace providers (businesses) government will be more efficient. Market-centric economics teaches that the market is more efficient than government (in part due to the presumptive "distortionary" effect of taxes). Even some public administration theorists, like James Q. Wilson, aver that the market is superior for achieving efficiency.[9]

Accordingly, the aim of government reformers has been to move an increasing share of government operations into the hands of business. Some cities boast of having only a handful of employees, as private companies run virtually all city services (Segal 2012; *Government Technology* 1995). And the Reinventing Government initiative of the Clinton administration set out to reduce the size of the federal government workforce by as much as 12 % (Moe 1994, pp. 114, 120) Which was done, according to congressional testimony in 2013 by Elaine Kamarck of the Brookings Institution, whose biography says she "created the National Performance Review" (the formal name of Clinton's Reinventing Government Initiative), and who boasted that "We reduced the federal workforce by 426,200 between January 1993 and September 2000. Cuts occurred in 13 out of 14 departments, making the federal government in 2000 the smallest government since Dwight D. Eisenhower was president" (Kamarck 2013, 2016).

Reducing the number of government employees, however, is not the same as reducing the size of government, especially when the reduction is achieved by contracting out. As Moe (1994, p. 120) told us:

> Equating the size of the federal government with the number of civil servants is a widely held, but misleading, belief and practice. In point of fact, the number of civil servants in the federal government relative to the overall U.S. work force, the fairest measure, has been steadily declining during the very period when the federal government has been accused of growing. In 1953, for instance, the federal work force as a percentage of the civilian work force stood at 3.48 % while in 1993 this percentage figure had fallen to 2.28 %, a decrease of 34.5 % during a period when the federal government was assigned many new functions (e.g., environmental protection).

> One misleading element in the linking of federal civil service totals to the size (whatever that term may mean) of government is that as the number of civil servants has decreased, the number of third-party personnel (principally contractor employees) has steadily increased…

In fact, "contracting out masks the true size of government" (Frederickson and Frederickson 2006, p. 21). Writing about the "true size of government" in 2002, Paul Light (2003) found that government grew overall but that the civil service was not the source. Federal civilian employment fell by 2.6 % between 1999 and 2002, while the number of private contractor employees grew by 16 %. As the Project on Government Oversight explained in 2012 (Amey 2012a): "The first myth of service contracting involves the notion that when the federal government outsources work to contractors, contractor employees are not part of 'big government.'…Because they are generally not seen as part of the total government workforce, they are spared the wrath of budget hawks calling for personnel reductions and cuts in

---

[9]Wilson (1989) writes: "If the preceding chapters have made nothing else clear, they should have persuaded the reader that government bureaus are less likely than private agencies to operate efficiently" (p. 349).

benefits. The number of contractor employees in the federal workforce is in excess of 7 million, nearly four times the size of the federal employee workforce." (Emphasis added).

Invisibility Is a Hallmark of Effectiveness

In the market, products and services are tangible and visible. When buyers purchase a good or service, they are aware of what they bought. In fact the market model is premised on the assumption that buyers have information about the product/service and know its price.

Many of the products of the public nonmarket, however, are intangible and often imperceptible, or are ubiquitous and taken for granted and therefore unseen. In many cases, the very *absence* of an undesirable condition (faulty wiring, contaminated food) is what government has produced.

Thus, when government is effective, its outputs and products may be largely invisible. People don't notice the absence of potholes, the fact their bank accounts are insured or street lights come on every night, the presence of clean air or potable water. They are unaware of the public R&D investments—paid for through their taxes—that led to the Google search algorithm and the technologies behind the iPhone (Mazzucato 2011; Upbin 2013; Jones 2013). And it is impossible for people to know about disasters that don't happen due to government action or intervention. Invisibility as effectiveness is one of the paradoxes of public goods.

Infrastructure in general is a product of government that is largely unseen, and underappreciated when effective. Infrastructure only becomes visible when it breaks down. Stephen Graham (2010) describes the invisibility of infrastructure in *Disrupted Cities: When Infrastructure Fails.* Citing Bowker and Star (1999), he notes that "good, usable [infrastructure] systems disappear almost by definition. The easier they are to use the harder they are to see. As well, most of the time, the bigger they are, the harder they are to see" (p. 6).

For Bowker and Star, one of the defining characteristics of infrastructure is that it "*Becomes visible upon breakdown.* The normally invisible quality of working infrastructure becomes visible when it breaks: the server is down, the bridge washes out, there is a power blackout" (p. 35).

Even innovation is invisible when it comes to infrastructure. Innovations that make bridges safer or longer lasting, roads ditto, electricity more reliable or public transit smoother go largely unnoticed. When public infrastructure agencies innovate and make things easier to use, those public goods become even more invisible, so innovation actually causes *greater* invisibility.

In *The Black Swan: The Impact of the Highly Improbable*, Nassim Taleb (2010) describes the paradox of the invisibility of disasters that don't happen. We don't know about some things government does "precisely because they were successful." "Assume," he says, "that a legislator with courage, influence, intellect and vision manages to enact a law that goes into effect...on September 10, 2001; it imposes the continuously locked bullet proof doors in every cockpit (at high cost to struggling airlines)…The person who imposed locks on cockpit doors gets no statues in public squares, not so much as a quick mention of his contribution in his obituary." On the contrary, "Seeing how superfluous his measure was, and how it squandered resources, the public, with great help from airline[s], might well boot him out of office" (p. xxvii).

The (Near) Inability to Measure What Matters

Measuring market success or failure is easy: a firm makes profits and stays in business; it goes into the red and it eventually dies (absent a government bail-out).

In the public nonmarket, nothing is so simple. The federal government itself has created two successive, massive performance measurement systems "GPRA" and "PART," but there is fairly broad agreement that these efforts (discussed below) have generally failed to deliver on their promises (e.g., Clark 2013, 2014; Radin 2011a; Anechiarico 2007; Joyce 2014). It is with regard to this inability to adequately, accurately, and meaningfully assess the results of public goods production, and to let the citizenry know what they want and need to know, that market model tenets fail most miserably.

The implementation of performance measurement in the public sector is advancing across government and through all levels of public education. Most readers, and much of the American public, are familiar with the measurement systems of No Child Left Behind and the Common Core standards in K-12 education. Few are aware of other massive performance measurement schemes imposed in the name of government accountability. In health care, the Senate passed legislation in April 2015 to revamp Medicare's payment system to pay doctors based on "performance" and "quality" of medical care—terms yet to be defined. In 2015 the Obama Administration attempted to roll out a new college rating and ranking system for all colleges and universities in the U.S., tied to federal student financial aid (Hernandez 2014). After an outcry from educators and universities, the ambitious plan was scaled back (Shear 2015) to a "scorecard." And despite the widely-publicized disasters of the Veterans Administration pay-for-performance system, it has neither been cancelled nor scaled back.

An entire industry dedicated to government performance measurement has spawned a vast literature on assessing processes and measuring results. Some of the key issues and problems have been commonly identified, others barely recognized. In *The Dynamics of Performance Management*, performance measurement expert Donald P. Moynihan (2008) cites numerous examples of how performance measurement programs and approaches have failed, asking if we've simply seen "Reform in Search of a Theory?" New performance management systems are repeatedly legislated without regard to the failures of past and present systems. And none takes into consideration the unique characteristics of the public non-market.

The persisting inability to measure and communicate the results of government production of goods and services underscores the need for a comprehensive economic model of the public nonmarket. Problems specific to performance measurement the *public non-market* include:

Goal Definition

Profit maximization is not—or should not be—the goal of government (though due to perversion of purpose, income generation is increasingly being set as a government ambition). If not profit, then what? Within the vast and growing performance measurement industry, hundreds of thousands, more likely millions, of "experts" have spent decades trying to figure out how to define public purpose, public value or to just define the goals of individual agencies or government programs.

Although performance measurement systems were initiated in the federal government during the late 1970s,[10] determined efforts to define goals began with the Reagan administration and its push for what it called "management improvement" (a name used to veil the actual intent of contracting out) (Kettl 1993, p. 43). In *Sharing Power* Kettl provides a mini-case-study in the complexity of goal definition in the public non-market as he describes the Reagan administration's struggles to define goals.

Their effort at goal definition ran into difficulties for a host of reasons unique to the public non-market. For example, the Reagan appointees had failed to appreciate that pursing "public goals as embodied in law…is the central task of government" (Kettl 1993, p. 40). In addition to the inherent complexities of defining public purpose. the Reagan administration had "efficiency" as its stated goal, and the notion of efficiency had to be rendered into something measurable. Kettl reports that it often took 18 months and sometimes two years to assemble the data required for performance criteria for required work statements. Not the embodiment of efficiency. This occurred in the 1980s, but as of yet, there still is no effective solution for the best way to go about identifying goals and setting measurable objectives.

Goal Ambiguity

The "Superfund" program offers an example of the ambiguity of many public sector goals. Created by legislation in 1980, during the last days of the Carter administration, the purpose of the program was to clean up toxic waste sites around the nation. But many questions arose. What is the definition of "toxic"? What is/is not a carcinogen? What were the guidelines for a safe and thorough clean-up? The ambiguities resulted in a ballooning of the projected number of sites that had to be cleaned up, from 400 initially to 378,000 by 1989.

---

[10]Specifically, as part of the Comprehensive Employment and Training Act under the U.S. Dept. of Labor, where I worked at the time.

Conflicting Goals

Public sector agencies are often handed conflicting goals in their authorizing legislation (see Radin 2012; Kettle 1993). One frequently-cited example is the Food and Drug Administration, mandated to approve only those drugs determined to be safe, but also to help "speed innovations" to market.

Invisibility

The paradox of invisibility as a hallmark of effectiveness (as discussed above) poses one of the largest problems in measuring results, yet is a hurdle scarcely recognized. How is it possible to measure the effectiveness of preventing disasters that do not happen? Perhaps a new kind of "counterfactual" approach is needed. Invisibility also presents a problem in terms of messaging what matters. It is possible to *measure* the quality of common and ubiquitous public goods such as safe, un-potholed streets, clean air and clean water, but the challenge is how to *message* the effectiveness of such products, given that they are only noticed upon breakdown.

The "Hollow-State" Problem

In their book about the problems of measuring results in the "hollow state," Frederickson and Frederickson surprisingly note that "most" of the programs and services of the federal government are now carried out by third parties. One of their main points is that the performance management systems that have been imposed on the federal government do not take this reality into account, since there "is an implicit assumption of direct government provision." But, because of widespread contracting-out, agencies are "being held responsible for performance of third parties over which they have limited control" (Frederickson and Frederickson 2006).

Multiple Entities to Satisfy

In the market, the producer/seller has only one entity to satisfy with its products: the customer who is buying. In the public nonmarket there are multiple entities to satisfy: (1) the recipients or beneficiaries of the public products or services; (2) the elected representatives in the legislature (Congress, state legislature or city/county council); and (3) voters. In addition, agencies must assess and communicate whether legislated purposes have been met. No performance measurement system, at least at the national level, addresses this complexity.

Opacity

Various types of opacity of the public nonmarket environment make it difficult for voters and taxpayers to appreciate the results of their electoral choices or to see what they have paid for through taxes.

- Obscured choice: Collective choice is a process with built-in opacity. Voters, the actual originators of the goods and services that the state provides, often do not "see" the real, practical impacts of their decisions. I.e., there is frequently a lack of visible connection between the act of voting and the results of the choices made. People cannot easily associate their choice of representatives with specific impacts on their daily lives.

- Obscured purchase: Public goods are paid for collectively, through taxes, a function that obscures the connection between payment and the thing purchased, in contrast to customers in the market who readily see what they buy (albeit, not the hidden defects in what they buy).

These forms of opacity mean that it is difficult to trace cause and effect for purposes of performance measurement. They also mean that extraordinary effort is required to communicate the results of electoral choices and collective payment to those who vote and who pay taxes. With few exceptions, such efforts are not made in the United States today.

The "Submerged State"

Some public products and services remain hidden by design, a deliberate strategy described by Cornell political scientist Suzanne Mettler in her critically important work on "the submerged state." In 2008, Mettler showed that although 96 % of Americans have participated in government programs, most surveyed deny it, insisting that they "have not used a government social program."[11] Among those who claimed they didn't get government benefits were 44 % of Social Security recipients, 43 % of unemployment insurance recipients, 53 % of federal student loan recipients and 60 % of those who took the home mortgage interest deduction. Mettler has argued that influential, private interests do not want people to know how much they are receiving from government. As Mettler writes, the state's role has been intentionally submerged and shrouded, "making it largely invisible to ordinary citizens."

A reviewer of Mettler's book, *The Submerged State: How Invisible Government Policies are Undermining American Democracy,* notes that "Opinion polling demonstrates that citizens are largely unaware of the existence of the submerged state; consequently they do not give government due credit for its intervention or hold it to account in an informed way" (Hackett 2012). Tax expenditure programs, in particular, "conceal the gears of government," a strategy looked to by Republicans and Democrats alike. Writing about Mettler's work, Eduardo Porter (2015) observes that "the strategy carries a cost. Such spending through the tax code not only offered the false promise of smaller government. Its most insidious effect was to hide what the government does and, notably, to shield from political debate which people it benefits most… Professor Mettler argues it has helped cement the image of a government that most Americans wrongly consider largely irrelevant to their lives."

---

[11]Mettler (2010). Mettler's 2012 *New York Times* Op Ed with John Sides, "We Are the 96 %" notes that the 4 % who have not used a government program are mostly young people who are not yet eligible for the benefit programs.

Tax Expenditures

Government programs that are funded through tax expenditures, rather than through appropriations, are effectively not subject to performance measurement. Tax expenditure programs comprise a mostly concealed, but enormous, part of the federal government (as I discuss in Chap. 5). Since 1994, the GAO has been urging Congress to include tax expenditure programs in its performance measurement requirements, to no avail. The GAO reported that "An estimated $1 trillion in revenue was forgone through tax expenditures in fiscal year 2011," but noted that federal agencies were not required by the Government Performance and Results Modernization Act of 2010[12] to include their tax expenditure programs. A 2013 GAO report (2013a, p. 15) concluded: "With so much spending going through the tax code in the form of tax expenditures, the need to determine whether this spending is achieving its purpose becomes more pressing."

Pay for Performance

Pay-for-performance schemes invariably fail to deliver the improvements intended; instead, they produce negative, and sometimes disastrous, unintended consequences, as I described in Chap. 2.

Measuring Long-Term Positive Externalities

Many public goods and services are created to produce long-term positive externalities. Public education, public health programs, clean air and clean water regulations, job-training and workforce development programs, early childhood education programs are but a few examples.

Only rarely have attempts been made to determine whether the intended, long-term results were achieved.[13]

Economist Jeffrey Sachs (2013) has called for "thinking long-term." In an Op Ed he reminded readers that "the United States government has a strong track record of success in long-term public-private investment programs. Federal agencies helped support and guide the birth of the computer age, the Internet, the Human Genome Project, the federal highway system, the GPS revolution, the global fight against AIDS and, of course, the space program." Sachs then (2014) advocated a "sustainable development economics" and public-private "complementarity" that would see public—along with private—investment in "infrastructure, human capital, intellectual capital, natural capital and social capital."

Interested private investors know how to evaluate such investments if made: did they produce a profit? But how will the public investments be evaluated? Will the goals of the public investment be in the public interest, unambiguously written,

---

[12]GPRAMA called for a "framework" for evaluating tax expenditure programs, but as of the 2013 GAO report, it had not been implemented.

[13]E.g., cost-benefit analyses of the Perry Preschool program in the 1990, which estimated levels of lifetime earnings and lifetime tax contributions, and, more recently, a study by Chetty et al. (2014) on teacher impact on long-term student outcomes.

clear and not conflicting, measurable? And how many years into the future will the long-term positive externalities of such public investments be measured?

Non-use of Results

Enormous effort has been made and many millions spent on public sector performance measurement at all levels of government. At the federal level, two massive government-wide programs were created—the Government Performance and Results Act (GPRA) of 1993, enacted concurrently with the Reinventing Government initiative of the Clinton administration, and the Program Assessment Rating Tool (PART), created in 2002 by the Bush administration. Then GPRA was amended by the GPRA Modernization Act (GPRAMA) of January 2010, signed by President Obama in January 2011.

Many studies have found that the results of these performance rating systems have gone unused by government managers for program improvement as well as by Congress when making funding decisions (Moynihan and Lavertu 2012; GAO 2014; Radin 2011b, 2012; Metzenbaum 2013, 2014; Frederickson and Frederickson 2006, p. 184). Clearly, these attempts to impose market-like "accountability" regimens on the public nonmarket have not delivered the promised market-like results.

This is hardly to say that performance measurement in the public domain cannot work. It can (as has been demonstrated in limited cases), and some believe it must (Ellig et al. 2011). But approaching performance measurement from the perspective of "accountability," and trying to mimic the market, is not the way to go about it.

Effects of Market-Mimicry

So let's look at some specific results of practices of market- mimicry in the public non-market economy.

De-democratization

The most corrosive aspect of the marketization of government occasioned by the New Public Management and Reinventing Government movements, backed by mainstream economics, is their threat to democratic governance.

Economist Servaas Storm (2015), crediting John Kenneth Galbraith, talked about the power of mainstream economics to "de-democratize" nation-states:

> By claiming that their economics has no content of power and politics but is neutral, mainstream economists have become "useful" as the influential and invaluable allies of the powers that be… They help de-democratize economic policy, which is quintessentially political and should be the subject of intense and informed democratic debate.

Ronald Moe and Laurence Lynn are two of a small cohort of analysts of public administration who have made the connection between government marketization and de-democratization and pointed to the threat the movement poses to our constitutional foundation for democracy.

Here is Moe (1994, pp. 114, 112), critiquing the Clinton/Gore initiative on "Reinventing Government":

> The [old] administrative management paradigm with its emphasis on the Constitution, statutory controls, hierarchical lines of responsibility to the President, distinctive legal character of the governmental and private sectors, and the need for a cadre of nonpartisan professional managers ultimately responsible not only to the President but to Congress as well is depicted as the paradigm that failed…[There has been] an intentional break in management philosophy from earlier organizational management studies going back to the Progressive Era and indeed, in a very real sense, back to the founding of the Republic. [Earlier reform movements] all emphasized the need for democratic accountability of departmental and agency officers to the President and his central management agencies and through these institutions to the Congress.

And here is Lynn (2001), critiquing New Public Management:

> Public administration as a profession, having let lapse the moral and intellectual authority conferred by its own traditions, mounts an unduly weak challenge to the superficial thinking and easy answers of the many new paradigms of governance and public service. As a result, literature and discourse too often lack the recognition that reformers of institutions and civic philosophies must show how the capacity to effect public purposes and accountability to the polity will be enhanced in a manner that comports with our Constitution and our republican institutions.

If the general failure to connect market-driven reforms with their impact on democratic governance is so obvious and fundamental a threat to our constitutional form of government, why has this impact been so overlooked in public administration scholarship and economics? The simple answer may be that it's no longer obvious, given the market triumphalism of the last half-century in the United States. A more sophisticated answer may be that, **in the absence of any adequate positive model of the public nonmarket, it is exceedingly difficult to explain and defend the dynamics of an economic domain that differ intrinsically from those of the market**.

A few political scientists, a few scholars of public administration, and a few economists have pointed out some of the ways in which the public domain differs from the market, specifically calling attention to the political process. Economist Richard Musgrave, writing in the mid 20th century and building upon the ideas of 19th–century European public finance scholars, argued that "A political process must be substituted for the market mechanism" in originating and allocating public goods and services (Albert and Hahnel 1990; Desmarais-Tremblay 2013. In the 1990s public administration scholars Stewart Ranson and John Stewart (1989, p. 7; also 1994) argued that public goods and services "are provided following a collective choice and financed by collective funds" and that collective choice is a process through which "differing interests are resolved, and conflict and argument lead to decision and action."

But the path laid by thinkers like Musgrave, Ranson and Stewart seems to have been cut short. In *Classics in the Theory of Public Finance*, Musgrave and Peacock excerpted the writings of early 20th century scholars of public finance, some of which hint at causes that may have contributed to its ending. (These authors used the terms "financial sociology" and "public finance"; they didn't speak of the public nonmarket.) German sociologist Rudolf Goldscheid, for example (1925/1958), said that "it is the most serious deficiency of our whole body of social science that we lack of a theory of financial sociology and that the problems of public finance remain without sociological foundation...[T]he science of public finance is that part of the social sciences which has lagged furthest behind during recent decades an which indeed is less advanced now than it was in the past." He cited as obstacles to the development of such a theory the rise both of socialism and of capitalism. "Marx so completely neglected the State in his conclusions that he failed to observe how its expropriation helped the private expropriators." As a consequence, "Capitalists have used the public household on the largest scale to enhance their profits and extend their power since capitalism has emerged triumphant in the form of finance capital."

Whatever the reason the path ended, we still lack a fully-drawn theory of how goods and services originate through collective choice in a democratic nation-state.[14] We need an economic theory that accounts for the public nonmarket mechanism by which the citizenry choose and pay collectively. We need a theory that recognizes the centrality of the election of representatives who legislate goods and services into being, and which lays out the forces that drive and constrain nonmarket production, including an explanation of effective and efficient production in the public nonmarket. The theory must recognize that this complex mechanism through which products and services are originated, and the public production process itself, rest on the foundation of the democratic process and constitutional governance. (See Chap. 5 for elements of such a theory.)

The Perversion of Purpose: Revenue-Raising Becomes a Goal

With the marketization of government, public agencies lose sight of their mission and turn to revenue-raising as a goal in and of itself. I described examples of this perversion of public purpose in Chap. 2.

---

[14]Note that, for those cited in the preceding two paragraphs, voting as collective choice stands in stark and important contrast to the market model's other and various explanations of collective choice.

Another example: in order to raise cash, cities are selling property tax liens to private debt collectors who can then legally foreclose, seize and sell property. Homeowners who are behind on tax payments, sometimes by only a few hundreds of dollars, have lost their homes due to such foreclosures (Hogan 2014) There are hundreds of examples of public agencies compelled or persuaded to make the pursuit of revenue their mission.

The Conversion of Citizens into "Customers"

The influence of mainstream economic thinking has fostered a market-myopic view not simply of the economy but of our society as a whole, especially in the US, where university students and hospital patients alike are now being re-branded as "customers." Use of the term has been enormously damaging. In a paper examining the effects of "economics-driven" political culture and public administration, Richard Box (1998, p. 38) warns that "Today's expansion of economic thinking and the potential separation of expert service provider (public service professional) from customer (citizen) may be one of the most serious threats to public service values Americans have experienced." And another paper on public sector "customer service" (Fountain 2001) finds that "customer service techniques and tools applied to government may lead to increased political inequality."

The Hollowing-Out of Government

The extent to which government has been hollowed-out is not fully appreciated by the public or by schools of public administration (Frederickson and Frederickson pp. 10, 152), whether we are speaking of the elimination of hundreds of thousands of civil service positions or the resultant incapacitation of remaining workers to effectively do their jobs.

According to research by the Project on Government Oversight (POGO) (Chassey and Amey 2011) "approximately one-quarter of all discretionary spending now goes to service contractors." POGO reports (Amey 2012a) that "The number of contractor employees in the federal workforce is in excess of 7 million, nearly four times the size of the federal employee workforce (which is over 2 million)."

The consequence of this transformation is not just a dwindling public staff but loss of a tradition of expertise and loss of institutional memory. Government is the most complex "conglomerate" in our economy, requiring a staggering variety of types of expertise. Consider, for example, the range and depth of expertise required for food and drug safety supervision and regulation; for banking supervision and regulation; for road construction and maintenance; for the operation of public health programs; for public transit maintenance of buses, trains, electric trams, rails, and power lines; for weather prediction; for pollution abatement and toxic waste clean-up.

When contractors take over the production or delivery of these goods or services, the relevant capability and expertise is transferred out of the public sector. Government loses its capability. This phenomenon is documented extensively in *Measuring the Performance of the Hollow State* (Frederickson and Frederickson 2006, pp. 2, 8, 152), who describe "what is now the dominant federal government approach to policy implementation—articulated vertical networks of third parties." They stress the enormity of the transformation to "third-party government" which has gone largely unnoticed even as it results in a thoroughgoing "redefinition of management and public administration. Much of what has traditionally been thought to be public administration, such as record keeping, hiring, promoting, supervising, contacting clients, budgeting, and the like, are now exported to third parties."

We do have a large corpus of studies on the results of contracting-out, which has swept through government at all levels. Despite the multitude of analyses (e.g., Sclar 2000; Mildred Warner 2011), insufficiently appreciated is the detrimental effect of contracting out not only on the provision of vital public services but on policy-making itself. When government employees cease doing the actual work of producing and delivering, they lose the knowledge, skills and expertise to develop sound policy and to oversee the substantive work of contractors. As James Galbraith (2008) shows, this effect is not unintended by the anti-government forces that promote privatization. The depletion of talent and expertise, and the resulting ineptitude, give further ammunition to those who advance privatization.

The Disregard of the Biophysical Aspects of Production

Just as mainstream economics ignores the existence of the public non-market economy, it disregards the biophysical basis of production (Hall et al. 2001), and the role of energy in particular. In *Energy and the Wealth of Nations*, Charles Hall and Kent Klitgaard (2012) show that economics for the most part has "treated energy not as a critical factor of production but only as another commodity to be bought and sold" (p. 8). They argue that treating natural resources and energy "simply as a commodity or as an externality" imperils future economic development, especially the prospects for sustainable development.

Market mimicry in the public domain exacerbates the depletion of natural resources and stymies a transition to renewable energy. If mainstream, market-based economics insists on disregarding the biophysical basis of production and development, certainly a new public economics cannot.

The Frustrated Quest for Efficiency

While constant allegations that government is inefficient have driven many government reforms on a quest for efficiency, no one agrees on how best to define "efficiency" in the public nonmarket. In Chap. 5, I list some of the attempts to arrive at a definition. Defining efficiency in the public nonmarket is a major unaddressed need.

Performance Measurement Practices Produce Unintended and Injurious Results

Government performance measurement systems repeatedly produce unintended consequences or fail to measure what is most important to citizens (Margetts et al. 2010; Radin 2006; Norman 2006). A notorious example is "No Child Left Behind." The distress over this ill-conceived measurement system and its successors continues, as teachers struggle to teach to the test while still hoping to provide students with the knowledge and skills that they will need in daily life. We've seen consequences of pay-for-performance at the Veterans Health Administration. And there is reason to be cautious about the "pay for performance" system of the Affordable Care Act, for we already have careful evidence from other countries that warns against medical pay-for-performance systems (Hartocollis 2013; Hood 2001; Dixon and Lodge 2012, p. 3).

Ill-devised or cynically-imposed performance measurement systems also produce gaming and subversion among staff penalized by the systems. One example is the VHA performance bonus scandal described in Chap. 2. But gaming of ill-designed systems is not uncommon, in either the private or public sectors. As Moynihan and Soss write (2014, pp. 328–29): "These sorts of bureaucratic responses are a staple of the literature on performance systems…[and may] represent forms of backlash and resistance or "may be 'rationally perverse' responses to the structures, pressures, and incentives created by the policy itself…They are administrative consequences of policy that merit theoretical and empirical attention as feedback effects."

Performance management can be a powerful driver for public programs and employees, for better or for worse. Among the growing army of private-for-profit consultants on performance management, *none seems to acknowledge that government operates in a non-market environment, and that government performance measurement needs to be rooted in an understanding of the dynamics of the public non-market.*

The Limitations of Markets

Neva Goodwin (2005) reminds us of "the limitations of markets":

> The free market model assumes that *markets exist for, and are used to allocate, everything that affects economic wellbeing.* That is, it is assumed that society relies completely on the market for all economically relevant resource allocation...[So] standard economic analysis only looks at that part of the world that operates through markets. This is one reason that its optimality predictions and prescriptions may not address the realities of the world we live in.

Certainly these "optimality predictions and prescriptions" do not address the realities of the public nonmarket, which significantly shapes the world in which we live. We need a less dogmatic and more sophisticated analysis of all that does not come within range of the market.

Chapter 5
The Public Economy: Elements of a New Theory

Crucially absent from current economic thinking and from current principles of public management is an understanding of the forces and dynamics of nonmarket production in the public economy. In order to revitalize the practice of public administration, we need a new conceptual framework: a model of the public non-market economy.

Imposing market axioms and precepts on the public non-market is not merely ineffective; it is too often disastrous, as I detailed in previous chapters. The market model wreaks havoc because it is neither apt to the public economy nor disposed to accommodate its intrinsic differences. As I enumerated earlier, the market model falls flat for important reasons specific to the public non-market, where

- The basic dynamic is not exchange: the producer does not sell and the recipient does not buy.
- Supply is free or with fees that are not economically significant.[1]
- Recipients pay collectively, before goods and services are even produced.
- Choice about what to produce is made collectively, emanating from the polity but as intermediated by elected representatives.
- Revenue is received from—or withheld by—elected officials; it does not come from "customers", no matter how well served or how satisfied recipients may be.
- The monopsonist is often powerless to dictate price.
- Invisibility of products and absence of problems are indicators of effectiveness and hallmarks of success.
- It is devilishly difficult, and has mostly proven impossible, to concur on and to measure what matters.

In this section I outline basic elements of the public nonmarket economy. I present a conceptual model of the forces and dynamics of production within this

---

[1]See definition of "prices that are not economically significant" in *NIPA Handbook—Bureau of Economic Analysis*, Nov. 2011.

© June A. Sekera 2016
J.A. Sekera, *The Public Economy in Crisis*,
SpringerBriefs in Economics, DOI 10.1007/978-3-319-40487-5_5

distinctive environment. I explain how these characteristics differ from the market model and why those differences matter.

The State as Producer

In grammar school we learn that government has three functions—legislative, executive and judicial. The function of the "Executive Branch," or so we are taught, is to carry out or enforce the laws passed by the Legislative Branch. However, the term "executive function" is misleading: it sells short what that branch of government actually does. In reality the function of the Executive Branch is largely *production* (with characteristics and dynamics much more complicated than those portrayed in the neoclassical economic model and its "production function").

Neither economics nor public administration theories adequately address the state's function as a producer. Neoclassical economic theory squints at government through the lens of "market failure," blind to government's presence as a legitimate economic producer in its own right. Tellingly, Adam Smith had a broader view of the functions of government than today's mainstream economics. He acknowledged that government's functions include providing education and building infrastructure, such as roads, bridges, and canals (Adam Smith cited in 2013). This role however has been conveniently forgotten by market advocates, while Marxist economists generally ignore the dynamics of non-market production by government in societies that are primarily market-based, concentrating instead on the stages and perils of capitalism. Political economists are concerned with the "powers" of the state and of its branches, rather than its function as producer.[2]

At heart, the field of public administration concerns the state but generally does not engage with concepts of public production. This avoidance is sometimes explicit and intentional.[3] In other cases it may be in order to keep econometricians from annexing the discipline. "The language of buyer and seller, producer and consumer, does not belong in the public domain," writes Marquand as quoted by Thomas Diefenbach (2009); "nor do the relationships which that language implies."

---

[2]For example, writing about "America in Decay," political economist Francis Fukuyama (2014) talks about "the executive branch that uses power to enforce rules and carry out policy."

[3]In an encyclopedia entry on NPM (Hood 2001), we find Christopher Hood a widely-cited scholar of NPM in Europe, writing that "Gregory's controversial claim that orthodox managerial approaches foster a 'production' approach to public services that leads to several unintended effects, including downgrading of responsibility and what he termed 'careful incompetence." It's not clear why a "production" approach is seen as the cause, rather than the market-centeredness of NPM. A similar avoidance of the economics of production may be found in Stephen Osborne's critique of NPM as overly reliant on product-focused management theory which has been derived from research on the manufacturing sector. But his focus (Stephen Osborne 2006) is on debates about administration versus management, products versus services, and intra- versus inter-organizational theory, all of which miss the critical issue of a destructive reliance, in actual government practice, on market-centric principles in the midst of a non-market.

This declaration misses the nub of the problem, which is to explain why the public economy, however much it produces, should never be presumed to operate like a market entity.

In reality, much of what the state does is carry out production. This is the case whether done directly by government employees or contracted out. In the public products economy, production is shared between the legislative branch (with its powers to *authorize and appropriate*) and the executive branch, which bears the responsibility for actually *producing* those goods, services, benefits and other products.

One of the few who has described the function of the state as producer, and did so eloquently, was Paul Studenski, a professor of economics at New York University (1927–54), an authority on public finance, and a frequently-cited historian of national income accounting.[4] I can do no better than to quote at length from his essay, "Government as a Producer" (Studenski 1939):

> In every type of political organization known in human history, from the most primitive to the most elaborate, government has had to furnish services satisfying important needs of the members of the society, help them to make a living, influence their productive processes and consumption habits, manage economic resources to these several ends, and generally function as the **collective economic agent of the people**. The productive character of government activity was recognized by political and economic philosophers from ancient times down to the earlier part of the modern era. [Emphasis added]

He then dissects the history and illogic of the "theory of non-productivity of government", as I quoted previously in Chap. 1. He not only shows the source of that illogic as embedded in unproven assertions of market superiority, he also challenges the supremacy bestowed upon individual choice:

> It is wrong to conceive of economic effort as being purely individual in character. **Under all forms of organized society, economic activity has required some collective effort in addition to the individual one, and this is still true of the modern society. The notion that production for exchange is alone "productive" is preposterous.** [Emphasis added]

> Production consists in the creation of utilities. Government furnishes services and goods which satisfy the two tests of economic value-namely, utility and scarcity. They satisfy human needs and must be economically used. Government is, therefore, engaged in production just as much as is private enterprise. Government employees are just as much producers as are private employees and entrepreneurs. To deny this fact is to demonstrate one's faulty economic education or the fact that one's idolatry for business has thwarted one's vision.

Now he lays out the differences between private market production and public non-market production:

> The productive activity of our society is divided into two main sectors-the private one in which production is carried on for profit and controlled by the forces of supply and demand

---

[4]In *The Income of Nations* (1958), Studenski traced the history of national income accounting and competing historical conceptions of production. Descriptions of Studenski's work can be found in Warren (2005) and Ogle (2000).

operating in the market, and the public one in which production is conducted for common advantage and is controlled by political forces. These two sectors of the national economy, commonly known as the "private economy" and the "public economy," complement each other, each serving different needs of society...

In the public economy...goods and services are produced which require the collaboration of all the members of society, and can generally be enjoyed by them only in common. They are largely intangible in nature, and in most cases cannot be divided into specific units and supplied to their users in that form. The services and goods produced in the public sector serve to maintain organized society... [including] protection of life and property, the administration of justice, and the regulation of economic activity...They also provide specific aids to private production, such as roads, and improvements of rivers and harbors...

...Obviously, without the services of government, society would be in a state of chaos and all production would stop....

Many economists and public policy scholars are now making the case that businesses need government in order to produce.[5] Although this is now a fashionable theme, it is hardly a new idea.

Equally important, if rarely discussed, is the fact that mainstream economics in general has historically dodged the matter of production, focusing instead on "exchange." Economist Michael Perelman (2006) has called attention to this fundamental evasion within contemporary economics and examined its origins. The mainstream focus on exchange seems to have been a reaction to Marx, whose "analysis of production could be turned to demonstrate how employers exploited their workers." In reaction, many economists in the later 19th century "felt a need to recast economics as a science of exchange rather than production." Moreover, an economics rooted in exchange is more amenable to mathematical modeling, a method that gained favor as the study of "political economy" was transformed into a social science of "economics," with increasing claims to quantitative exactness. So today we have an orthodox economics that focuses on "exchange" within "the market," thus setting up a model in which the state has no legitimate role as a producer.

"Market Failure" Is not the Justification for the Public Economy

As Polanyi (and others) have told us, society is not a market; rather, governments *enable* markets. But most contemporary economics teaching ignores the fact that the state is a legitimate producer in its own right. The legitimacy of the state as producer is not, and should not be, dependent on a concept of "market failure," a concept launched so successfully by Francis Bator (writes Wentzel 2011) that it has become "one of the most generative ideas (theoretically and empirically) to emerge

---

[5]For example, see Sachs 2014 and Jan W. Rivkin, Michael E. Porter, Rosabeth Moss Kanter, David A. Moss, in "Can America Compete?" *Harvard Magazine*, Sept.-Oct. 2012, pp. 26–43.

from economic theory." Wentzel, however remains skeptical, for acceding to the argument that "The state is necessary because markets fail…plays into the hands of the libertarians, as the debate is implicitly based on the core libertarian assumption that such a thing as a 'free' market can exist."

The Public Economy and Popular Sovereignty

As taught today in most universities, economics elaborates on concepts about markets that originated centuries ago in an age of mercantilism and monarchies. Forms of societal organization have since evolved—most notably with the development of democratic nation-states. Conventional economics has not kept up. To be sure, other theories and models have appeared: Marxist, Keynesian, feminist, behavioral…. Yet in Western democracies the ancient model reigns. And not only are we taught that it accurately describes markets; it must also be applicable to government. In fact—in historical fact, economic fact—it doesn't. Many have come to think that it no longer works well even with regard to markets. However that may be, the historical, economic, and political reality is that the market model's precepts and axioms are regularly imposed on government at every level. This misapplication of antique theory is no mere problem of intellectual dissonance, sloth, or dishonesty; it's a recipe for disaster.

We lack a theory that reflects reality. In reality government is a producer. A workable theory of the public economy needs to explain how government production occurs. It must address two questions. First, what is the source of the public economy's ability to produce—that is, what is the source of its power? Next, where does it get its resources—its inputs for production?

For answers we must acknowledge the contributions of political science, as well as the historical school of economics, which holds that economic systems are related to, and differ by, various forms of societal organization.[6,7] From political science we have the concept of "popular sovereignty," upon which modern democracies are grounded, and wherein the power to act emanates from "the People" and flows from them through a constitution to that organization called

---

[6]While my thesis and conceptual model are not derived from the historical school, it is important to recognize this non-orthodox, non-mainstream perspective that, while alive for a while, seems to have been extinguished. In his book on the Historical School, Shionoya (2005) writes both of its importance and of its dismissal by orthodoxy: "The German Historical School, belonging to the tradition of historicism as part of German romanticism and idealism, wrought a radical transformation in the outlook of economics. Yet mainstream economics has never taken the impact of the [Historical School] seriously…." Yuichi Shionoya, *The Soul of the German Historical School; Methodological Essays on Schmoller, Weber, and Schumpeter*, Springer, Boston 2005, p. xiv.

[7]For a relevant and cogent analysis of the nature and functions of organizations see Domhoff (2005), who holds that "organizations are the starting point for understanding power."

"government."[8] In effect, in democratic nation-states, popular sovereignty creates a collective sovereign.[9]

To carry out the will of the collective sovereign, government must produce goods and services. While political science addresses the origin and delegation of *political* power (the power to make law), it does not address the origin and delegation of *economic* power, specifically, the "power to produce." An economic theory is required to explain and illuminate the dynamics and drivers of the environment in which government, using collective inputs, is able to produce.

The Public Economy in the Scheme of Things

While mainstream economics teaches that government—the agent of the unacknowledged public economy—is legitimate only where there is market failure, the reality is that government precedes the market, historically and conceptually. Governments existed before capitalism and before any theory of markets. Moreover, laws and public services must exist in order for markets to function at all. In effect, society enables markets, not the other way around. Indeed, as Braudel argued half a century ago,[10] there are multiple economies, not just a single, market economy. In addition to the public economy, we can speak of two other non-market

---

[8]In the framing of the US Constitution there was great debate about where sovereignty lay, whether with the federal government or the individual states. Ultimately it was decided that sovereignty rests with the People (Ellis 2015; Verkuil 2007, pp. 15, 81, 102). The original, late medieval concept of popular sovereignty was not directly associated with democracy, given that the concept of "democracy" itself was not held in high regard. Indeed, writes Ellis, "the term democracy remained an epithet until the third decade of the nineteenth century. It meant mob rule, the manipulation of majority opinion by demagogues, and shortsighted political initiatives on behalf of the putative 'people' that ran counter to the long-term interests of the 'public.'" With the passage of time, however, it has become widely accepted that popular sovereignty is the bedrock of the US Constitution and government, as well as of other democratic nation-states. Yet the embrace of popular sovereignty does not of itself yield a thoroughly democratic system. As even Wikipedia reminds us, "In most modern democracies, the whole body of eligible citizens remains the sovereign power but political power is exercised indirectly through elected representatives." Moreover, these days the ability of the people to exercise their sovereignty is being severely undermined (Verkuil 2007; Dahl and Soss 2012; Moe 1994; Lynn 2001). And as Susan George observes in *Shadow Sovereigns* (2015), "transnational" corporations have overturned democratically-enacted laws in order to pursue their own profit-maximizing ends.

[9]Although this Brief treats democracies, I would argue that my approach holds for those many nation-states organized under other systems of government. Wherever there is a public economy (and that would include all, or nearly all, nation-states), the market model is inadequate for understanding or explaining it. There is a need, rather, for a theory of public economics that identifies and takes into consideration the sovereign source of the power to produce, as well as the source(s) of the inputs for production, regardless of the system of government.

[10]Fernand Braudel (1981) *The Structures of Everyday Life. Civilization and Capitalism*. Volume 1; cited in *The End of the Experiment; From competition to the foundational economy*; Andrew Bowman et al. (2014, pp. 12, 116–118).

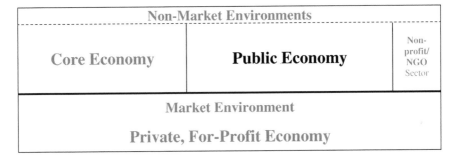

Fig. 5.1 Multiple economies

environments: the "core economy" and the non-profit sector. By far the larger is the core economy (Goodwin et al. 2014, pp. 64–67), representing the productive, unpaid, activity of households (notably not counted in calculating GDP). The core economy supplies the market economy with resources (e.g., labor) and demand. The other non-market environment is the non-profit or NGO community.

Thus, the non-market economy has three components: the public economy, the core economy; and the non-profit sector (Fig. 5.1).

The market economy could not exist without the core economy and the public economy. And it could not function absent the outputs of governments. Market-based businesses require such public goods and services as property protection, contract law, patent protection, communication and transportation infrastructure, as well as scores of other public products. Corporations owe their very existence to the public, collective sovereign, and derive their legal protections therefrom. But the public and core economies can, and historically did, operate without the market economy.

The Public Non-market Economy

The public nonmarket is that part of the public economy in which the production of goods, services and other products is capitalized collectively (through taxes), and is empowered through collective choice (voting), and in which products are provided free or below cost at the point of receipt or usage. In the U.S., the public non-market economy includes government operations at all levels—federal, state and local. The public non-market, in the conceptual model described in this section, does not include "government enterprises"—public entities that charge prices sufficient to cover the full cost of production. My thesis is concerned only with the public *non-market*. (It is important to recognize, however, that some public agencies have been transformed by changing their mission from meeting a public need to revenue generation, which leads to their characterization as "government enterprises" and inclusion as "businesses" for purposes of national income accounting.[11] One such example is the U.S. Post Office (Backman 2012; Hamilton 2012; Jamiel 2014; Brechin 2014; Nixon 2013. See sidebar).

Government Enterprises that Aren't

Market advocates have transformed some public agencies into "government enterprises" by changing their purpose from meeting a public need into revenue generation. An example of this is the Post Office, a public service specifically enumerated in the Constitution, and which throughout most of its history was supported by collective payment (in addition to nominal fees). But the Post Office was re-defined by market advocates in Congress who succeeded in passing legislation in 1970 that required the (renamed) "US Postal Service" to cover all expenses through revenue generation. Having succeeded in transforming its driving force from public service to revenue production, these marketizers in 2006 imposed an artificial debt burden on the new entity so that it would become impossible to cover costs.

Elements of the Public Non-market

The public nonmarket economy differs from the market model on fundamental and crucial factors, which I detail in this section:

- Purpose: need-driven, not demand- or profit-driven.
- Systemic driver: collective choice, electorally manifested.
- Source of income: collective payment, not payment via exchange.

I then draw out particular features of the public nonmarket:

- Flow relationships and dynamics
- Agents in the generation, creation and production of public products
- Unique factors of public non-market production:

  votes as an input resource
  authority to enforce as a unique asset
  natural resources and energy: the public role

---

[11] Arguably, a number of public agencies, such as public transit and local housing authorities, have been mis-classified by the National Income and Product Accounts (NIPA) used for calculating GDP. Because they are defined as "government enterprises", they are defined as "businesses" in NIPA accounting and their value added is recorded in the "business sector" for GDP purposes (Baker and Kelly 2008).

- Unique supply conditions: required rationing
- Unique products
- Public goods
- Expenditure without spending
- The absence of buyers
- Non-market efficiency
- Invisibility as a hallmark of effectiveness
- Non-rival supply
- The uncommon complexity of judging results.

In each instance, I explain how these characteristics differ from the market model and why those differences matter.

Purpose: Meeting a Societal Need, not Maximizing Profit

The fundamental purpose of public nonmarket production is to meet the unmet needs of a society[12]: to supply goods or services not supplied by other means, to solve difficult and complex social or economic problems, or to make goods or services accessible to all, regardless of ability to pay (Wuyts 1992; Desai 2003; Ranson and Stewart 1989, pp. 10, 12, 24; Galbraith 1958, p. 242), In many cases, the intent is to create positive externalities, sometimes immediate and sometimes long-term.[13]

In the market, access to products and services is expressly contingent on ability to pay. In the public non-market, supply is free or with fees that are not economically significant.[14]

It is axiomatic that non-market production is not about producing income or profit. "Societies run at a loss so that their citizens can live at a profit, in productive comfort" (Gopnik 2013).

Note that, though the goal of revenue-raising to cover the costs of production is inimical to the inherent purpose of public goods production,[15] as government is marketized there are constant demands to increase fees in order to replace collective payment.[16]

---

[12]Note that "needs" includes the needs of people, organizations, businesses, communities or the natural environment.

[13]Weisbrod (1964) in an analysis of the long-term impacts of public education, makes the point that "when goods and services have significant external effects the private market is inadequate".

[14]See definition of "prices that are not economically significant" in *NIPA Handbook—Bureau of Economic Analysis*, Nov. 2011.

[15]The only justification to make revenue-raising a goal is to raise money to cross-subsidize the supply of other public goods.

[16]And of course, some public services, like the Post Office, have been required to cover all costs with revenues, tossing out the concepts of collective payment and universal access.

Need-Driven, not Demand-Driven

Non-market production is need-driven, not demand-driven.[17] In the public non-market, needs are articulated and become a systemic driver through the process of electorally-manifested collective choice.

Electorally-Manifested Collective Choice

In the public non-market, collective choice replaces market "demand." Public, non-market goods and services originate through the complex process of collective choice in the polity—i.e., voting. Voting, and hence democracy, is the "process by which individual choices are socially structured" (Gutmann 1987, p. 134, quoted by French 1998, p. 339).

In the real world, electorally-manifested collective choice is the generative source of public products. Public products are not created in response to demand. Instead, a variety of products—goods, services, benefits, and obligations—originate from the complex decision-making dynamics of collective choice and collective payment. This is in contrast to the relatively much simpler "supply" and "demand" dynamic of the market environment.

Mainstream economics has not offered a useful analysis of collective choice for purposes of understanding the public non-market, particularly that collective choice is the originating driver of the public production process. The topic is usually treated from a theoretical perspective, grounded in assumptions of the market model. No consideration is given to voting as a *resource input* for public production, and how this input impacts on the production process itself.

Of course, "public choice" economics addresses collective choice, but this school of economics is indentured to the market paradigm and does not look at how collective decision-making through voting eventuates in the production of public goods and services.

Methodologically individualistic, public choice economics maps a set of individual preference orders onto a social preference order (Wolff 2010). Public choice economics treats the concept of collective choice from an exclusively theoretical perspective, addressing questions of how collective decisions may be made. In their critique of public choice theory, Stretton and Orchard (1994, p. 124) ask: "Why theorize so artificially when political life is accessible to more direct study? From studying the theorists' activity we have come to believe that many of them chiefly want to discredit government, but that for many of them a main purpose is to develop theory of a certain formal kind for its own sake, and to debate and elaborate

---

[17]Wuyts (1992), but cf. the work of economist Geoffrey Hodgson (2013), who distinguishes "needs" from "demand," which is a function of preferences and the ability to pay (Tankersley 2014, p. 671).

its internal forms as an acceptable academic activity." (For more on collective choice and public choice theory, see Chap. 6).

"Social choice" theory has been another avenue by which mainstream economists address collective choice. This theory, too, disregards the real-world operation of electoral collective choice and its impact on the public economy. As Stretton and Orchard observe (1994, p. 57), "Leading social choice theorists claim to be broadly concerned with the relation between citizens' individual judgments and their collective social decisions, a subject which has occupied political philosophers since Plato." In fact, these theorists have been "narrowly concerned with some logical qualities of sets of individual preferences, and with the impossibility of deriving collective preferences from them by mathematical procedures."

One of the most prominent theorists, Kenneth Arrow, produced an "elegant" formulation that came to be known as "Arrow's Impossibility Theorem," which demonstrated that a mathematics of ideal societal choice was unattainable. "There the business ought to have ended," write Stretton and Orchard (1994). "…[I]nstead an extraordinary thing happened. The search for a consensus machine did effectively cease, but forty years and a thousand books and articles later, scores of economists are still writing variations of Arrow's work." To compound the problem, "The theories which Arrow showed to be impossible, and most of the impossibility theorems themselves, are concerned with attempts to arrive at social policies without considering their effects" (pp. 57–60).

Amartya Sen, the other major contributor to the mathematics of social choice theory, has been truly concerned with the effects of social choices. Still, his work addresses the question of how best collective choice *should* be carried out. He does not investigate the implications of real-world, electorally-manifested collective choice for a public non-market environment.

Few economists have allowed the political process of collective choice to be seen as a legitimate replacement for the market concept of demand. One exception is Richard Musgrave:

> Since the market mechanism fails to reveal consumer preferences in social wants, it may be asked what mechanism there is by which the government can determine the extent to which resources should be released for the satisfaction of such wants…A political process must be substituted for the market mechanism.[18]

Musgrave (1956/57, p. 335) cites Swedish economist, Knut Wicksell, who earlier made the same point (albeit still holding onto the superiority of market-modeled individual choice):

> Wicksell…noted that *a political process of decision* making must be substituted and enforced. Since decision by voting will hardly be unanimous, the result will not be optimal. However, the voting mechanism must be designed so as to approximate a true statement of

---

[18]The quote is from Michael Albert and Robin Hahnel, "A Quiet Revolution In Welfare Economics", but Maxime Desmarais-Tremblay (2013) provides a more extensive analysis of Musgrave's work.

preferences, and hence come as close as possible to that solution which would be obtained if the exclusion principle and the forces of the market could be applied.

In the 1990s public administration scholars Stewart Ranson and John Stewart (1989, p. 10) weighed in:

> ...choice has to be made from a number of competing claims. There will be arguments about needs, spillovers, rights and obligations. Collective choice is political because *these disagreements and conflicts of interest have to be resolved before social life can proceed.* Collective conflict has to resolve into collective choice. [My emphasis.]

Writing about "shared social responsibility," political sociologist Claus Offe (2010, p. 95) makes a similar point today. He talks about "self-binding acts of pre-commitment: at their origin stands the political, collectively binding *choice*, made in the past by some winning coalition of political forces."

Perhaps a useful way to think about the function of collective choice in economics terms is to see it as societal choice about the combination of outputs on the Production Possibilities Frontier (PPF). Societal choice answers the rhetorical question that economics does not:

> What precise combination of outputs, such as guns and butter, or health care and highways, should society choose to produce? The PPF does *not* answer this question. The [PPF] curve shows the range of efficient possibilities, but does not tell us which one of these combinations of outputs is best... In a society with free speech and democratic discussion, there is wide room for disagreement about what the best mix of goods might be. The PPF provides a mental image for thinking about scarcity, tradeoffs, and efficiency but does not, itself, tell us how to choose among the possibilities it illustrates (Goodwin et al. 2015 Chap. 2, p. 8)

Neither economics nor economists can tell us what combination of outputs a society should choose, but in terms of public goods, a democratic society makes its choices by the representatives its citizens elect.[19]

Does voting "work"? Scholars, activists, political leaders and media critics have wrestled with this question, since voting often appears to disappoint as an effective mechanism for the expression of collective choice. Too many don't vote; elections are bought by those with the most money; those who would like to vote are denied the ballot by technical but discriminatory measures.

But the question at hand is not whether voting works. For better or worse, voting is how, in reality, collective choice is manifested in a democracy.

It is crucial that we better understand the role of voting (real-world collective choice) in producing public goods and services. An understanding of how voting is central to economic collective choice has been impaired, and its centrality obscured, by neoliberals and the political right, which insist on the priority and superiority of individual choice, as taught by mainstream economics. Whether in the guise of public choice economics, Arrow's Impossibility Theorem, the writings of Coase or

---

[19]Tocqueville in *Democracy in America* p. 59, quoted by Beryl Radin (2012, p. 9) said that in the United States "The nation participates in the making of its laws by the choice of its legislators, and the execution of them by the choice of agents of the executive government...The people reign in the American political world as the Deity does in the universe".

Hayek, or strands of rational choice theory, mainstream economics has exhibited an elemental "hostility to democracy"—and here I am quoting an economic historian, Philip Mirowski.[20]

Although rarely characterized as such, economic attacks on government are really attacks on democracy, and a devaluing of electorally-expressed collective choice. Before we can act as a society to clear the way toward effective voting, we must therefore shape a valid theory of public goods provision in the public economy. Only then will we have an intellectual infrastructure that demonstrates that the public goods economy is not only viable but vital.

Collective Payment

In the market model, individual buyers pay; collective payment is not recognized or accounted for in market "exchange". While mainstream economics discusses taxes at length and speculates about their influence on individual behavior and their "distortion" of market activity, it does not deal with the implications of collective payment, or what might be better called "collective purchase," on non-market production.

Collective purchase is an extraordinarily complex process entailing distinct acts by different groups of agents. In contrast to utility-maximizing individual choice and payment in the market, payment for goods and services in the public non-market originates collectively—through taxes. Purchasers—taxpayers—do not pay the producer directly.[21] This single fact introduces a complexity into public production that does not exist in the market: a third-party agent (legislature, city council, Congress), who actually supplies money to the producer so it can produce. Once payments from individual taxpayers have been aggregated, the pooled financial resources are put to use only after a process of legislative appropriation.

The complexity of collective payment has consequences not found in the market:

- Payers are often unaware of what they have "bought" with their tax payments.
- The size of the producer's budget is determined by elected intermediaries; it does not grow or shrink based on effectiveness or customer satisfaction.

  In contrast, the market mechanism for payment (from buyers) and income (to producers) is simple: payment is made directly to the seller/producer: and satisfied buyers are the source of a firm's income. So the size of a firm's budget is a function of payments from buyers.

---

[20]Mirowski (2015) was pointing principally to microeconomics, but he implied that the charge could also be levied against aspects of macroeconomics.

[21]Any fees that may be paid by users are not, or should not be, intended to cover the costs of production.

Collective payment means that the size of a public agency's budget is not determined by satisfied clients, users or recipients of services or goods. Rather, payment by the buyer (taxpayers) becomes income to producers (public agencies) only and always at the discretion of elected representatives. Thus, income to the producer is *not* connected to effectiveness: whether recipients/users are satisfied or dissatisfied, or whether the specified public need has been met is, by and large, unconnected to whether the producer receives income. Income to the producer may be terminated even when production has been effective, the public need is being met and the recipients of goods and services are satisfied. Conversely, funding may continue even if the identified need is not being met.

Such dynamics and un-market-like incentives are usually cited as symptoms of the "dysfunction" of government. But it is time to stop squinting at the public sector through a market lens and to see public production as a valid economic process. Only then will it be possible to appreciate that the dynamics of the public non-market are not necessarily dysfunctional but essentially different. It is high time that we arrive at an understanding of how non-market dynamics and incentives operate. At that point, we can establish operational methods of governance that produce desired results.

Flow Relationships and Dynamics: A Conceptual Model

The market is a two-way exchange; the nonmarket is a three-node production flow.

Consider my diagram below comparing the dynamics of market and nonmarket environments. The market is an *exchange*: a producer sells and a buyer buys. But there is no such "exchange" in a non-market production environment. Instead, there is a *flow of actions among agents in a system of production*, in which acts or outcomes are contingent upon prior acts or outcomes, ultimately relying on the polity. Public goods are created through legislation, by legislators whose existence is contingent upon voters. The flow of funding to the producer is contingent upon elected representatives. The source of financing, collective payment (taxes), is contingent on the vagaries of the tax system, politics and the health of the economy. Finally (and problematically), recipients of public goods are often unaware of their source. Making the connection between payment (taxes) and receipt of goods, services and benefits is contingent on making them visible through public messaging (which, for many public goods, is never done) (Fig. 5.2).

Separate Agents for Generation, Creation and Production

In the market model, the producer/seller determines what goods or services to supply, obtains resource inputs and can choose to continue producing a particular

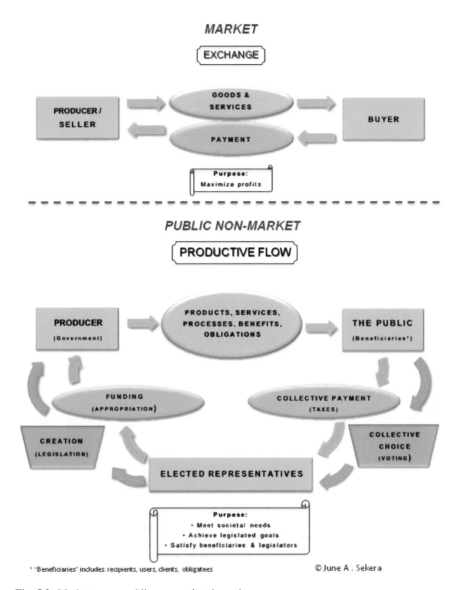

Fig. 5.2 Market versus public non-market dynamics

good or service as long as the price that has been set continues to attract customers willing to pay. The producer or seller (or its investors) can also choose to stop producing if profits are insufficient. In effect, the firm plays the roles of generator, creator and producer of goods or services.

Generation	→	Voting and taxes (collective choice and collective payment)
Creation	→	Legislation (write, promulgate, pass). Two separate steps —authorization and appropriation
Production	→	Public agency produces It either delivers directly or contracts out and oversees

Fig. 5.3 Origins of goods and services in the public non-market

In the public non-market, the *generation*, *creation*, and *production* of goods and services are separate acts by different groups of agents. The roles of the agents are as follows.

Generation—by voters
Goods and services are *generated* through collective choice, i.e., the complex process of collective decision-making (citizen voting) and collective payment. Demand in terms of individual desire, willingness and ability to pay is inoperative.

Creation—by Legislators
In the market, goods and services originate with the same entity that produces them: the firm decides what to produce, how much to produce and how to capitalize production. That's not true for the public non-market, where the entity (the public agency) that produces goods and services does not create them in the sense of either inspiration or capitalization. Legislators. rather than the public agency-producer, determine *what* specific goods or services to produce, and whether to increase or decrease the level of production. Although public goods in essence originate with citizens when they vote for their representatives and are paid for collectively through taxes, it is the elected intermediaries who make day-to-day decisions about how and when collectively-raised monies will be used. They determine what will be created, how much will be produced, and when and whether to initiate, continue or terminate particular goods and services.

The *creation* of goods and services takes place through the process of writing, promulgating and passing legislation. And there are two separate types of legislation that must be passed—authorization and appropriation. Not infrequently, goods and services are "authorized"—through authorizing legislation—but no money is appropriated. So, while authorized, many times they are not, in fact, created.

Production—by public agencies
The public agencies of the "executive" branch are the producers.[22] Public agencies use a variety of inputs—labor, capital, talent, technology—to produce scores of types of outputs (infrastructure, a system of education, a stable currency system, and regulations that protect people and businesses and scores more) (Fig. 5.3).

The dynamics among these agents are intrinsically different from, and far more complex than, market dynamics (as diagrammed in Fig. 5.2).

---

[22]It doesn't matter, in this context, whether the public agency contracts out. Even if it does, it is still the producer—i.e., it is responsible for what gets produced.

Input Factors—Resources to Deploy

Votes: An Input Resource

According to rational-choice theory–a theory central to mainstream economics–voting is an irrational act. Based on analyses of marginal costs and benefits, the effort (cost) required to vote in elections far exceeds the likelihood that an individual's vote will affect the outcome (benefit). Putting aside the invalidity of this assertion from a psychological/sociological perspective (see, e.g., *Economist* 2012; Barro 2014), textbook characterizations of voting as irrational, repeated for decades, undermine the legitimacy of the public domain. If taken to heart by the general population, such characterizations would threaten the very foundation of democracy.

Unfortunately, this characterization is endemic not only to economics but to some schools of political science as well. Gerry Mackie (2011), one of the few in the field to have thrown a spotlight on this development, has traced the process through which political science was "overtaken" by "the economic theory of democracy." As the field adopted mathematical modeling, some embraced the mathematics of rational-choice economics that showed voting to be "arbitrary and meaningless." Since then, much of political science has been part of a "stampede away from voting" and toward debates about "deliberative" democracy, to such a degree that now "Voting, oddly enough, is one of the least active areas in political theory." In a delicious passage, Mackie finds that "Voting has the same relationship to deliberation in much deliberationist theory as sex has to love in the Victorian marriage: it is necessary, frequent, of profound result, but is suspect and mentioned only in fleeting allusion."

Given the cost-benefit conclusion that voting is irrational, and its outcomes arbitrary and meaningless, Mackie sums up the inevitable conclusion: "democracy should be minimized and the market maximized." And indeed, public choice economics views voting exclusively from the vantage point of market exchange: politicians "buy" votes to stay in office via the positions they take and policies they support.

Certainly, elected officials endorse policies and vote for legislation in ways that gain them political support and additional years in office, but they also (and often) vote with the public interest in mind. Further, whatever the role of selfishness may be in all human affairs, rational-choice assumptions about the electorate or its elected officials shed no light on the ongoing dynamics of how public goods and services are actually produced.

I offer a different proposition: votes are an input resource. In the public non-market, like land, labor or capital, votes are an input to production.

The textbook definition of production is "the conversion of resources into goods and services" (Goodwin et al. 2014, p. 46).

Among the resources used in production is "social capital," defined as: "the institutions and the stock of trust, mutual understanding, shared values, and socially held knowledge that facilitates the social coordination of economic activity."

I submit that votes are a social capital resource. Votes are perhaps the most fundamental and essential resource of the public economy, though rarely if ever recognized as such in economics.

It is important to note that, in the public non-market model, votes are not equivalent to "demand" in the market model. Indeed, there is no "demand" in the public non-market environment, just as there is no "exchange" but rather a productive and contingent flow as shown in Fig. 5.2. Public goods and services originate through collective choice—i.e., voting, in democratic societies—and votes (along with taxes) generate goods and services through the actions of elected representatives. Here is Stiglitz:

> In the public sector, choices are made *collectively*. Collective choices are the choices that a society must make together...Unlike expenditures on conventional private goods, which are determined through the price system, expenditures on public goods are determined through a political process....Individuals vote for elected representatives, these elected representatives in turn vote for a public budget, and the money itself is spent by a variety of administrative agencies.[23]

If individuals and societies engage in managing their resources, and if collective choice (along with collective payment) generates the production of goods and services in the public domain, then votes are an input resource.

Authority to Enforce: An Asset

In the market model, firms have a variety of assets to deploy, including financial and human capital and technology. The public non-market producer has all of these resources and (as Mark Moore writes), an additional unique asset: the legal authority of the state to enforce.[24] In democratic nation-states, this authority derives from collective choice expressed via democratic electoral processes (Ranson and Stewart 1989, p. 20).

The legal authority to enforce enables the state to produce outputs that the market cannot or does not, such as clean air and clean water regulation, food safety

---

[23]Stiglitz (2000, pp. 15, 156–57). Although Stiglitz gives a rhetorical nod to collective decision-making through the political process, he reverts to standard economics modeling, using the "collective demand curve," to explain what he calls "the demand" for public goods.

[24]The idea that the state has a monopoly on the power to legitimately use force is generally credited to Weber's theory of the state as developed in a lecture, "Politics as a Vocation" (Weber 1919). For a discussion of the implications and impact of the substantial differences between the assets of the private sector and the assets of the state, see Moore (2014).

standards, bank regulation, product safety recalls, contract and property rights enforcement. The deployment of this unique asset[25] results in the production of an obligation, and those covered become "obligatees" (Moore 2014, p. 470), as I discuss below.

Natural Resources and Energy: The Public Role

As I noted in Chap. 4, mainstream economics neglects the biophysical basis of production and slights the significance of energy in particular.

A new public economics cannot make the same mistakes. Taking the lead from Hall and Klitgaard (2012), it must be "a *biophysical* science that reflects the actual conditions in real-world economies." A new public economics must appreciate natural resources, and energy in particular, as a special category of inputs to production, not mere commodities to be purchased and exploited. Further, a public economics must recognize that electorally manifested collective action is the only means through which democratic societies can protect and preserve natural resources and usher in a societally-beneficial transformation to renewable energy sources.

Supply Conditions

Required Rationing

In the market, the financial capital for production comes from savings, from equity or debt investments, or from sales in going concerns. Firms making profits attract investors. Kenneth Arrow (1963) explains, "In competitive theory, the supply of a commodity is governed by the net return from its production compared with the return derivable from the use of the same resource elsewhere." But, as he points out, "There are several significant departures from this theory" in the supply of some "commodities" (e.g., medical care), which don't conform to the market model (p. 952).

Nor does public non-market production. While a firm's ability to attract capital is governed by its return from production, in the non-market the producer's supply of financial capital is circumscribed by the collective payment process. The government producer has little or no control over its supply of capital, and therefore no control over the quantity of a good or service that can be produced. Normally, in the public nonmarket, the need is greater than the resources made available to the producer through legislative appropriations. The result is rationing.

---

[25]For a discussion of the assets of the private sector vs the state and the impacts and implications of these differences, see Moore (2014).

The public non-market producer cannot increase its capital, and hence its capacity to produce, by obtaining money from satisfied customers. Instead, as a standard matter of practice, it must ration its supply of goods and services. And if funding is cut, the result is closed parks, limited library hours, and the declining capability of the National Weather Service to predict storms or tornadoes.[26]

In theories of government and public administration, rationing, which goes on in the best of times, is a virtually ignored factor of production from the perspective I have just described (Stewart interview 1994), although it is a daily feature of operations in producing many public goods and services.[27,28]

Mainstream economists characterize rationing quite differently. In *The Economics of the Public Sector*, Stiglitz describes rationing as a response to public economy "overconsumption": "Given the inefficiencies arising from overconsumption when no charges are imposed…governments often try to find some way of limiting consumption". This is a doubly distorted reading of the situation: it blames the victim—i.e., those in need of public goods or services (as, for example, a college education); it leads one to think that government agencies have a choice about how much to supply.

What public servants actually face is what John Stewart has called "the management of rationing": how to make services go as far as possible within externally-imposed budget controls.[29]

Products

Goods, Services, Processes, Financial Security, Obligations

The public non-market produces products—or outputs—that the market does not. And those that are particular to the public non-market are arguably more complex (Fig. 5.4).

With the exception of obligations and processes, these categories are fairly self-explanatory.

---

[26]Concerning the consequences of cutting the budget of the National Weather Service, see Doswell and Brooks (1998), Sirota (2013), Miles (2014) and Anyone regret slashing National Weather Service budget now?; *Salon*; Tuesday, May 21, 2013.

[27]An operational definition is needed for the term "rationing" in the context of the public non-market environment. Cf. Ubel and Goold (1998).

[28]In the public non-market, it may well be that need always exceeds supply, so that no equilibrium can be reached. If so, the theory of equilibrium may be another conventional market construct that is inapplicable to the environment of non-market production.

[29]A useful discussion of the dilemmas of rationing, and sometimes tragic choices, faced by public sector producers can be found in an article on health care rationing by Ubel and Goold (1998).

Market	Public Non-Market	
Category	Category	A few examples of public non-market products
Goods	Goods	street lighting; sidewalks; roads; nautical navigation markers; clean water; parks; playgrounds; currency; bridges, dams, canals, dikes, airports, shipping ports.
Services	Services	food safety inspection; 911 call service; mail delivery; weather forecasting; natural disaster prediction; disaster response/relief; education; bank deposit insurance; job training programs, patent system; enterprise and socioeconomic data collection and dissemination; innovation through basic R&D investments.
	Processes	legal / judicial system; copyright enforcement; infrastructure maintenance and repair.
	Financial security	unemployment insurance; old age, survivors and disability insurance; pensions insurance.
	Obligations	drug safety regulation; product safety standards; water quality standards; emissions regulations; banking regulation; food nutritional labeling.

Fig. 5.4 Products of the market versus the public non-market

Obligations

Obligations arise from a resource unique to the state: the legal authority to enforce.[30] As with other public goods and services, producing these obligations entails collective choice, legislation, appropriation and administration.

There has been an astonishingly successful movement to force all who work in the public sector to use the word "customer" when referring to those who are, in truth, recipients, users, or beneficiaries. This market rhetoric, which has writhed across the public domain, cripples as it distorts, for the public economy is not a market; no one receiving or using public goods or services is a directly-paying, utility-maximizing buyer; and, most critically, much of what the public domain produces is obligations. It is absurd to claim that such obligatees as auto companies facing product recalls, corporations fined for emitting toxins, banks charged with consumer fraud, or criminals facing prosecution are "customers." Making public sector activities into a world of "customer" relations demotes or dismisses the role of government as an enforcer of societal values embodied in law. Which perhaps is not unintentional.

Processes

From the chart above, I choose to focus on infrastructure as a process. A similar argument can be made for the legal/judicial system.

In his essay, "When Infrastructures Fail," Stephen Graham (2009, pp. 9–10) makes a persuasive case that infrastructure networks are not so much products as processes:

> ...infrastructure networks, despite their occasional veneer of permanence, stability, and ubiquity, are never structures that are given in the order of things. Instead of being static

---

[30]For more on the concept of obligations as a "product" of government, see Moore (2014).

material or technical artifacts to be relied on without much thought, infrastructure networks are, in effect, *processes* that have to be worked toward. The dynamic achievement of a functioning energy, communications, water, or transport network requires constant effort to maintain the functioning system.

Infrastructure, writes Graham, is a "precarious achievement." Maintaining infrastructural services is a "constant process" calling into being a "vast and hidden economy of repair and maintenance [that] is continually at work to allow infrastructural circuits to actually work."

> Constituting at least 10 percent of most urban economies, this economy of repair and improvisation is almost invisible within the debates of urban studies. The sheer amount of economic activity generated by repair and maintenance is notable, even though it is almost completely ignored in accounts of the economies of contemporary cities. In the United States, for example, there were fully 5.82 million people engaged in installation, maintenance and repair (IMR) occupations in 2000 with a then-expected growth rate of 11.4 percent. These jobs constituted 4 percent of all jobs in the United States, making the sector one of the six most important service industry occupational groups.[31]

The invisibility of infrastructure, particularly when it is working properly—the paradox of invisibility—is emblematic of many other public goods and services.

Public Goods

The terms public good, public goods and public interest are often used interchangeably, without definition and without clarity. It is time that we pause over these terms and distinguish their meanings. In particular, in economics it is important to focus on the concept of public goods, and, I would argue, re-think the definition.

Mainstream economic theory, using the sixty-year-old formulation of Paul Samuelson, holds that public goods arise out of, and represent, "market failure." In the market-centric world of mainstream economics, public goods are pronounced "a problem" because, being "non-rivalrous" and "non-excludable,"[32] they are not amenable to market production.

The definition of public goods is little discussed by pluralist or heterodox economists. Instead, attending to the topic are those on the right who challenge the definition as too supportive of a role for government. Libertarian essays and websites question whether public goods actually exist—or argue that if they do exist, they can and should be provided by the market, not government. This literature supports the increasing marketization and privatization of government.

---

[31]Graham does not specify how much of this is public infrastructure. From the context it appears that it may be the majority.

[32]In mainstream economics a good is nonexcludable if the supplier cannot prevent consumption by people who do not pay for it and non-rival if more than one person can consume the good at the same time (Krugman and Wells 2009).

Cornes and Sandler (1994) nicely captured the situation when they asked "Are Public Goods Myths?" So far as they could tell, "Samuelson's austere simplification produced a rarefied concept, a mythical beast, without any counterpart in, and therefore without any applicability to, the real world" (p. 369). Because the Samuelson definition is so narrow and constricting, one can indeed demonstrate that the standard textbook examples of Samuelson public goods have been or may be produced by the private market: shipowners have paid for lighthouse services; monarchs have hired mercenary armies; Disneyworld produces fireworks. Even clean air is being purchased individually–by the wealthy in Beijing.[33]

In "Rethinking the Definition of 'Public Goods'" (Sekera 2014), I briefly review the historical development of the economics definition of public goods and suggest a path to re-conceptualization.

Expenditure Without Spending

In the market model, the source of financial capital for production is money in the form of cash, debt or equity investments. Simply put, the firm has or gets money and spends it to produce goods or services. However, in the public non-market, outputs can be produced and goal achievement accomplished through "tax expenditures" (tax credits, exclusions and other legislated forms of tax exemption financing) wherein the producer—a government agency—makes no outlay of money.

Tax expenditures are rarely thought of as a financing source for production of goods and services. But, as noted by Marr et al. (2013) of the Center for Budget and Policy Priorities (CBPP), "The distinction between tax breaks and spending is often artificial and without economic basis." The Joint Committee on Taxation (2014, p. 2) explains that "Special income tax provisions are referred to as tax expenditures because they may be analogous to direct outlay programs and may be considered alternative means of accomplishing similar budget policy objectives." Wikipedia (2015) is most blunt: "A tax expenditure program is government spending through the tax code."

Tax expenditures have been used to finance a large array of public products or benefits, including education, health care, business expansion, and home ownership. Marr et al. (2013) revealed that in 2011 tax expenditures ($1.072 trillion) cost more annually than either Social Security ($725 billion) or Medicare ($755 billion).

In his 1988 public economics textbook[34] Stiglitz noted that "We call these implicit grants tax expenditures. The federal government is required to make estimates of the tax revenue losses associated with each tax expenditure. In recent years they have become very large." Tax expenditures are enormous; for some public sectors they dwarf direct expenditures. The following chart is from Stiglitz (Fig. 5.5).

---

[33]In China in response to extreme air pollution, some schools have built domes over sports fields and wealthy parents choose schools based on air-filtration systems: Wong (2013).

[34]I did not find similar information in Stiglitz (2000). This chart is from the 2nd edition, Stiglitz (1988, p. 30).

Budget function	Direct Federal outlays	Revenue loss estimates for Tax Expenditures	Tax Expenditures as a % of Direct Outlays
Commerce	2.6	140.4	5,400%
Housing credit	1.9	44.3	2,300%
Health	106.1	31.4	30%
Income security	318.6	95.3	30%
General purpose fiscal assistance to state and local government	6.4	35.5	550%
Education, training, employment & social services	30.6	28.7	94%

Fig. 5.5 Federal tax expenditures: the major recipients, 1986 (in billions of dollars)

The House and Senate Joint Committee on Taxation report of August 5, 2014 lists 222 tax expenditure programs. For two comparable categories, the 2014 projected *revenue losses due to tax expenditures*—i.e., the costs to the federal government of these tax expenditure programs—are nearly triple what they were in 1988:

- Housing: $130.9 billion (as compared to $44.3 billion in 1988)
- General purpose fiscal assistance to state and local government: $92.6 billion (as compared to $35.5 billion in 1988).

Few taxpayers appreciate how well hidden are such expenditures, and how deceptive. As Stiglitz (1988, p. 30) commented, "Many government subsidies show up in neither the statistics on government expenditures nor those on tax expenditures." And a paper by the Congressional Research Service (Labonte 2010) explains that

> Because tax provisions are permanent (unless they include an expiration date), however, revenue loss from specific expenditures may rise over time automatically without congressional action, unlike appropriated spending. If this equivalence argument is correct, measures of the size of government that omit tax expenditures drastically underestimate its size.

As for deception, the Tax Policy Center[35] notes that tax expenditures "give the appearance of reducing government's size... In fact, however, tax expenditures can actually expand government's interference (sic) in the economy, partly because they induce changes in taxpayers' behavior. *Also, like direct spending, tax*

---

[35]http://www.taxpolicycenter.org/briefing-book/background/expenditures/controversial.cfm.

expenditures must also be paid for through higher taxes elsewhere." [Emphasis added].

In their study, "Government Spending Under Cover," Batchelder and Toder (2010) argue that tax expenditures should be called "IRS-administered spending programs." And they point out that "No one asks what goal a spending program dressed up as 'a middle-class tax cut' serves because it seems self-evidently good to give people tax cuts."

Another little-noted feature of tax expenditure programs is their tax impact when reduced or cancelled. Reducing or eliminating direct expenditure programs equates to a tax cut; eliminating tax expenditure programs equates to a tax increase. Annie Lowrey (2013) has shown how important this is for the public budget and public perception. Senator Patty Murray, observing that "We don't often think of tax expenditures as a form of spending," shepherded a budget proposal to raise nearly $1 trillion over 10 years by cutting tax expenditures, with the aim of using the new revenue to reduce the deficit. The attempt failed. Rep. Paul Ryan insisted that any money generated from curbing tax expenditures must be offset with lower tax rates and Sen. Jeff Sessions charged that "Eliminating tax exemptions is a tax increase. You can't spin it any other way."

The Absence of Buyers

In Chap. 4 I described the absence of buyers in the public nonmarket. Instead, there is a "purchasing agent", which is an organization (department, bureau) within the government. The prior discussion is summarized in this chart (Fig. 5.6).

	Market	**Public non-market**
Who purchases?	Buyer	Purchasing Agent
Why?	Self-interest	Meet a public need
With what?	Own money	Taxpayer money
Beneficiary	Self	People, businesses, organizations, communities, the nation, the environment, the planet.

Fig. 5.6 Payment: market versus non-market

Non-market Efficiency

So far as I can tell, we have no operational definition of efficiency appropriate to a non-market environment, particularly the public economy. We rely mistakenly (Reinhardt 2010) on market criteria of efficiency (and "Pareto efficiency").

I do find smatterings of recognition that the non-market environment complicates the notion of efficiency. A European Central Bank paper on public sector efficiency notes that "The concept of efficiency finds a prominent place in the study of the spending and taxing activities of governments." However, "The adequate measurement of public sector efficiency is a difficult empirical issue and the literature on it...is rather scarce. The measurement of the costs of public activities, the identification of goals and the assessment of efficiency via appropriate cost and outcome measures of public policies are very thorny issues" (Afonso et al. 2006, pp. 7, 8).

And a European Commission paper on measuring efficiency in the public sector (Mandl et al. 2008) notes that "Problems arise because public spending has multiple objectives and because public sector outputs are often not sold on the market which implies that price data is not available and that the output cannot be quantified (p. 2)."

A few other groups and individuals have argued that collective production and payment can be more efficient than market exchange and competition. But these too generally have retained market criteria for public production, despite the fact that, as the Oxford economist Avner Offer (2012, p. 2) points out:

> It has never been proven that markets always provide the most efficient economic outcomes; it is not even easy to determine what such efficiency would consist of. People often make choices which are not intended to maximise their economic advantage...Those who buy and sell for their own advantage, have no incentive to seek overall efficiency, and efficiency does not just happen by itself.

A major challenge in developing a theory of the public economy is to determine how to define and measure efficiency in a non-market environment.

Invisibility as a Hallmark of Effectiveness

The challenge of assessing effectiveness in the public non-market economy is formidable for many reasons, but I want to draw attention to two that usually go unrecognized: invisibility and opacity.

As I have already noted, public goods and services are created to meet the unmet needs of a society or to solve complex social or economic problems. When the needs are met or problems solved, they "vanish"; public goods, services and processes become invisible when successfully produced and provided. Where not invisible, they may be opaque: that is, taxpayers cannot easily or directly see what they have paid for.

Paradoxically, as Stephen Graham (2009) most graphically describes, many public goods and services are generally noticed only when they cease to be available, when they break down, or when an entire system fails for want of financing or manpower (as I summarized earlier). "When anthropologists or sociologists define the term *infrastructure*, the ways in which it sometimes attains cultural invisibility over time is one of the key criteria that they settle on." (p. 7)

The result is an "absence of presence" of public goods—what taxes pay for—in the minds of a mostly oblivious U.S. population. Earlier I summarized research by Suzanne Mettler (2010) at Cornell which showed that although virtually all Americans have participated in government programs, most deny it. As Mettler writes, the state's role—and thus the existence of public goods—has been intentionally submerged and shrouded, "making it largely invisible to ordinary citizens."

Also invisible is protection of the commons. In *Silent Theft*, (2002), David Bollier talks about how the commons—those natural goods and public assets that it is government's job to protect—are in our midst but unseen. He argues that we ignore the commons at our peril. "Why does the commons live in the shadows, virtually ignored?" Answering his own question, he says: "It is not easy to connect the dots among these complicated, seemingly unrelated events and recognize the larger pattern of enclosure...Learning to see and understand the dozens of commons in our very midst is one of the preeminent challenges of our times" (pp. 5, 6, 15).

Perhaps the most confounding type of invisibility in the public economy is the "product" of harm prevention: the disasters, illnesses or accidents that don't happen (because government has done its job). How can we gauge the effectiveness or efficiency of public agencies—producers—that daily and continually protect people, communities, and businesses from damage and harm?

Non-rival Supply

The economist Dean Baker has observed (2014) that "there is a real cost of using selfishness as a fundamental political principle." In effect, he was complementing what Will Davies (2014a, b) had written about the dangers of accepting "competitiveness" as a guiding societal value, and what Alfie Kohn (1986) wrote decades earlier in *No Contest: The Case Against Competition*.

Instead of the "competition prescription," a theory of the public non-market must recognize that a fundamental aspect of public supply is that it is non-rival. In public, non-rival supply:

- Producers strive to supply their goods or service to as many recipients or beneficiaries as appropriated funding will allow and as cost-effectively as possible;
- Producers share information and innovation freely with other producers in order to make the whole system more effective and efficient (rather than withholding "competitive, trade secrets" as in the market and, increasingly, in marketized government);
- There is a concern for citizens' welfare—rather than "buyer beware"—an environment of trust[36];
- The role of the federal government is to assist state and local governments, not to compete with them or put them out of business as competitors [in contrast to the now-popular idea of the "competitive state," which "concentrates political capital behind the *most competitive* cities, clusters and regions" and abandons "uncompetitive" places and populations—Davies (2014a, p. 146)].

The concept of non-rivalry in supplying public goods and services does not mean that there is no dissension, disputation or debate. Quite the opposite. But the disputation is built into the *generation* of public goods, up front, during the process of collective choice, not during the process of supply. To reprise Stewart and Ranson (1989) on this point:

> ...choice has to be made from a number of competing claims. There will be arguments about needs, spillovers, rights and obligations. Collective choice is political because these disagreements and conflicts of interest have to be resolved before social life can proceed. Collective conflict has to resolve into collective choice...The essential task of the public domain [is] enabling authoritative public choice about collective activity and purpose. In short, it is about clarifying, constituting and achieving public purpose (p. 10).

The collective choice process, through representative democratic government, resolves precisely *what* goods, services, benefits and obligations will be produced by public agencies. Once resolved in the form of signed legislation, public agencies must produce them, but they do so in a non-market, non-rival[37] environment, unless market principles are imposed and such marketization induces rivalry.

---

[36]Kenneth J. Arrow (1963) makes this point with regard to non-market medical care. A doctor's "behavior is supposed to be governed by a concern for the customer's welfare which would not be expected of a salesman."

[37]Those familiar with the textbook definition of public goods will recognize the term "non-rival" as an ascribed attribute. However, I use the term "non-rival" differently—as an attribute of the *process* of production, not of the goods produced.

Uncommon Complexity of Judging Results

We lack a framework for evaluating outcomes in the uniquely complex environment of public non-market production with its distinctive set of driving forces and dynamic flow relationships as well as its multiple constituencies. Performance measurement systems transplanted from business or designed by market advocates don't translate to the non-market. Such systems frequently backfire with unintended consequences. Federal performance measurement systems have been implemented without any grounding in a theory or concept of non-market production and have often been imposed for ideological, pro- and faux-market reasons. Simply put, the US has no appropriate performance measurement or performance management system.[38]

We do need and must have, in the public sector, a way to know if we're doing the right thing and doing the thing right. Lacking an apt method for measuring results, one that recognizes and comprehends the public non-market, we will continue to see failures.

What Must Be Addressed in Constructing a Means for Assessing Non-market Results

I turn now to specifics in order to arrive at a rational and useful approach for measurement of results in a public non-market. I take up in turn each of the unique features of non-market production that I have previously discussed.

Multiple constituencies

In the market, there is only one constituency to satisfy: customers.[39]

But in the public non-market, there are multiple constituencies to satisfy: (1) the recipients of the goods or services; (2) the elected representatives who appropriate the funding; and (3) the public (voters and tax payers). Additionally, the legislated purpose must be met. And beyond immediate outcomes, long-term impacts (intended positive externalities) should ideally be measured (Fig. 5.7).

---

[38]There is a small but substantial and growing literature on this deficiency. Numbers of individual agencies and programs have constructed effective performance measurement and management systems, and some are statewide. But these operate despite the imposition of ineffective or counterproductive federal performance measurement systems.

[39]Of course, investors must be satisfied with their return on investment, but that is a completely different point than the reality that buyers must be satisfied with the products or services that are produced, or revenues will cease.

MEASURES OF SUCCESS	
Market	**Public Non-Market**

Profit.
 	
(Of course there are investors and ROI, but if the business can't satisfy customers and sell its products , it ultimately ceases to exist.)
	1. **Whether the specified public need was met.** (i.e. the specific purpose for which the good, service, obligation or process was legislatively created) including:
	    a. **Short term outcomes; and**
	    b. **Short & long-term positive externalities.**
	2. **Satisfaction of recipients/beneficiaries.**
	3. **Satisfaction of elected representatives.**
	4. **Satisfaction of the public (voters/taxpayers).**

Fig. 5.7 Measures of success

The challenge is to find an *effective* way to measure whether the identified need has been met and the other criteria have been satisfied.

Connection to purpose

Since public goods, services and other products are created legislatively to meet identified public needs, the most elemental assessment determines the extent to which that need has been met. This is not straightforward. Exactly how do you measure the achievement of public purpose?

In the United States today, the purposes of public products are often ill-defined in their authorizing legislation. Moreover, a single piece of legislation or a single public agency may have multiple missions, sometimes conflicting (Radin 2012). That complexity of mission must not be dodged but addressed head-on in any attempt to devise a cogent approach to the measurement of results.

Satisfaction

In the past several decades, one of the principal thrusts of performance measurement systems, having been designed with the market as a model, has been to measure "customer satisfaction." While it is inarguably important to do a good job for clients of public services and users of public goods, the marketized approach is inappropriate for several reasons. Chief among these is that "many government activities do not involve the supply of services or benefits. When the government acts to protect citizens from criminals, to clean the air and water, and to protect those who are vulnerable in market transactions, it often acts not by providing benefits to particular individuals but by imposing burdens on those who threaten those individuals" (Moore 2014, p. 469). What is the logic of measuring the "satisfaction" of those on whom the "burdens" have been imposed? And how does one measure the impact of government obligations?

Dealing with invisibility

With regard to results measurement, the paradox of invisibility of public goods raises two types of questions: How do you measure what *is not* seen? How do you measure what *cannot be* seen?

In the first case—what *is not* seen—I am referring to such things as the absence of crime, the absence of toxins in food, water, and air. These public products can in fact be measured if standards have been set and published—standards of purity of water, for example—or by tracking the number of robberies, or illnesses or fatalities caused by tainted food. The problem in this case is making the public aware of what government has accomplished and driving home the direct connection between such desirable accomplishments and the payment of taxes. *Measuring* is not so much the problem; *messaging* is.

The case of what *cannot be* seen, of harm that does not happen, is much more difficult. Yet, a large part of government's mission is to protect and preserve, i.e., prevent harm from happening. The conundrum: how to measure disasters that did not happen, the absence of fatalities from food poisoning, bodies that have not been maimed by unsafe tools, illnesses that were not contracted...

Perhaps it is possible to re-think the concept of counter-factual impact evaluation. And, here again, is the issue of *messaging* government's accomplishments in having prevented harms.

Measurement of expenditures with no spending

Performance measurement has not been rigorously applied to tax expenditure programs. For example, Good Jobs First, an organization that tracks the impacts of "economic development" tax credits has spent years publicizing the "job creation", and actually the lack thereof, resulting from tax credits that are given to businesses. Though job-generation promises are rarely met in these programs (Story 2012), few legislators have heeded the findings.[40] In the "measure mania" that has been sweeping the nation as part of the government reform movement, it is hard to find attention being paid to the failure to measure outcomes of tax expenditure programs. Since 1994 GAO has been urging Congress to require that tax expenditure programs be subject to performance evaluation, without success.

Measure positive externalities

An unstated but prime intent of many public goods and services is to create positive externalities. Basic education is a fine example. Once a private service, it became public when voters decided—through their elected representatives—that every person should have free access to education, regardless of ability to pay. Though the immediate goal was literacy for all, there were other results too. As David Moss of the Harvard Business School has pointed out (2012, p. 42), the U.S. free public education system established in the 19th century, "financed by taxes rather than private tuition," represented "the virtual socialization of an industry. It was enormously controversial. Ultimately, though, the rise of public education constituted a powerful competitive advantage because it moved the United States far ahead of most other countries in terms of education and human capital development."

Public education is meant to do more than enable students to acquire literacy skills, get a job, or even to advance national competitiveness. It enables critical thinking and equips citizens to be informed participants in democracy. Similarly, clean air and clean water regulation, workforce training and public parks are meant to contribute to the overall and long-term well being of people, communities and

---

[40]In a partial victory, and as a result of the work by Good Jobs First, state and local governments that provide economic development tax credits will now have to publicly account for the losses. http://www.goodjobsfirst.org/gasb.

the planet, i.e., to create "positive externalities." Burton Weisbrod (1964), one of the few economists who have recognized the need to evaluate the creation of long-term externalities, published a report on the *External Benefits of Education* over fifty years ago. Yet no performance measurement schemes practiced in the U.S. today[41] consider long-term externality creation.

Advocating "sustainable economic development," Jeffrey Sachs (2013) tells us to "think long-term" about public investments, citing government accomplishments such as the federal highway system, the development of computers, the Internet and other technologies, and space exploration. If each of the programs that generated these accomplishments had been subjected to the type of market-myopic performance measurement system imposed on K-12 education over the last decade, would we have seen such long-term public investment? Without being able to see and measure the long-term positive externalities that have accrued to our society, would these programs have been sustained? Not likely. Economists such as Weisbrod should be enlisted to help develop ways to measure positive externalities, not theoretically, but in actual effect.

Conclusion

A theory of the public nonmarket economy, and a model of its production dynamics, must take into consideration all of the aspects discussed above. It must offer a clear, comprehensive explanation of the three-node flow of the public economy environment and recognize the contingent nature of each of the functions. It must—in any democratic nation—acknowledge that public products originate with the polity and that accountability is at the ballot box.

A theory of the public nonmarket economy must also relate to, and lay a clear and cogent foundation for, the practice of public administration. If our societies continue to have nation-states, we need to work out a better way to run them. Listen to Dwight Waldo (Lowery 2001), who was a leading 20th century scholar of American public administration:

> What we shall be able to achieve in the enterprise we call civilization is going to depend on increased understanding of formal organizations and, through increased understanding, increasing mastery.

---

[41]Note that in this section I am discussing the ongoing, growing and increasingly routine practice of "performance measurement" throughout government. This type of post-production measurement within and by government agencies themselves, but imposed from the outside, is different from third-party evaluations, which sometimes do attempt to predict or measure externalities, albeit usually not long-term ones.

Chapter 6
An Absence of Theory

Governments are not market institutions. That may seem obvious. Why, then, does economics have no analysis of this non-market system of production, no explanation for how it works, and so no understanding of the fundamental forces that govern the public economy? There is a void. This conceptual vacuum with regard to non-market dynamics has not drawn the interest even of heterodox economists; instead, it has invited neoclassical claims that market principles do, or should, govern the public economy. This in turn has opened the barn door to the marketization of government.

As I've endeavored to show, there are real-world consequences to marketization, with its flanking political and academic attacks on government. The significance of electoral collective choice is devalued even as the practice of government is undermined, with operational infrastructures dismantled and the public sector hollowed out and depleted of skills, talent, experience and institutional memory. In the wake are devastating consequences for the well-being of the citizenry, the economy, democracy, and the natural environment.

As Karl Polyani (1944) taught, society creates markets; markets do not create society. Government enables markets; markets do not enable government. But what has been insufficiently recognized and inadequately addressed is that government itself is a productive economic agent that operates in a non-market environment.

More than a century ago, particularly in Europe, the public economy was a significant concern of economics. However, with the insurgence of market-centric economics and ideologies, the public economy was exiled, first from the thinking of economics and then from public administration, until the very idea of a public non-market environment disappeared from sight.

Neither neoclassical nor Marxist nor feminist economists currently deal with the empirical reality of the dynamics and forces that drive and constrain the non-market public economy and production within it. Nor do behavioral or institutional economics. Public choice theory, to which many contemporary economists default for analysis of the public economy, draws its lifeblood from market-centric ideology and represents generally anti-public values and precepts.

© June A. Sekera 2016
J.A. Sekera, *The Public Economy in Crisis*,
SpringerBriefs in Economics, DOI 10.1007/978-3-319-40487-5_6

An Overview of the Historical Literature

The following is a brief historical overview of the disappearance of the public non-market economy as a concern of the literature of economics and the parallel literature of public administration.

Economics Literature

- In 18th- and 19th-, century Germany, economics and public administration were housed under the same rubric, *Kameralwissenschaft* ("Cameralism"), which an historian of economics, Roger Backhouse (2002, p. 166), describes as the era's "science of economic administration." The science had three components: public finance, economics, and public policy, each defined somewhat differently than we do now. While German universities established academic chairs in *Kameralwissenschaft*, there was debate about its diverse ambitions.

  According to economic historian Bruce Caldwell (2004, pp. 42–43), Cameralism as a form of administrative economics was meant "to assist the ruler of a state and the associated civil bureaucracy to govern wisely." However, "At the very point at which the Cameralistic sciences were at last gaining acceptance as a university discipline, they were displaced by a new form of economic reasoning. Economic teaching in universities was henceforth the province of a new *Nationalökonomie* which emphasized the economic activity and needs of the individual as the founding moment of the economic order, and not the activity of government over populations of territorial states."
- The "Historical School" of economics, which emerged in 19th-century Germany, viewed government positively as a system for promoting social well-being (Bogart 1939; Shionoya 2005) It stopped short, however, of explaining the operational or production aspects of the system.
- During the late 19th and early 20th centuries, economists wrestled with the question of how the "public economy" operates. A "voluntary exchange theory of public economy" was advanced by Emil Sax, DeViti De Marco, Kurt Wicksell and Erik Lindahl. During the 1940s–50s, Richard Musgrave argued against the voluntary exchange concept and pursued a line of thinking that eventually led to the construction of a concept of "public goods" that was eventually adopted, mathematicized and popularized by Samuelson (Desmarais-Tremblay 2013). Samuelson's widely-disseminated 1950s formulation of public goods as stemming from market failure (following Musgrave) soon led to their devaluation, and a wholesale devaluation of government, by market centrists and libertarians, eventually by all tributaries of mainstream economics. What had begun as a serious effort to understand the important role of public sector production ended in its willful neglect.

- In an important paper, Roger Backhouse (2005) describes the "profound changes in economic theory" that took place between 1970 and 2000. With the triumph of rational-choice economics came "a radical shift of worldview" and a "remarkable and dramatic change in attitudes toward the role of the state in economic activity." The rise of "free market" economics and the "ideology of rational choice" created a "climate of opinion" that seriously biased economics against government and led to a view the state as an agent whose actions lead to perverse outcomes. As Backhouse shows, however, "the shift toward market solutions did not occur spontaneously: it was actively promoted by groups of economists committed to opposing socialism [and] making the case for free enterprise."
- Tracing in greater detail the rise of rational-choice theory after World War II, Sonja Amadae (2003) explains how the theory had "profound implications for democratic theory." Claiming that "rational individuals do not cooperate to achieve common goals unless coerced," the theory's treatment of human rationality "could be used as a virtual litmus test to determine if one were a liberal individualist or an irrational collectivist" (p. 3).
- In his landmark book, *A Perilous Progress: Economists and Public Purpose in Twentieth-Century America* (2001), Michael Bernstein explores the evolution of economics from an academic field marginal to public policy into a powerhouse influencing and orienting government decision-making. Economists in the late 19th and early 20th centuries ardently sought to cultivate influence with elected and appointed officials to shape public policy and contribute to "purposeful management" and "statecraft." These were among the driving ambitions of the economists who led the American Economics Association after its founding in 1885. Seeking respect for economics as a new "scientific" field (no longer framed philosophically as "political economy"), "scholars sought a privileged and powerful access to public policy debate, formulation and implementation." Though they claimed the discipline had a legitimate role in statecraft, the influential Cambridge University economist Arthur C. Pigou had asserted in 1922 that it was not the business of economists to tell businessmen how to run their companies. Advising on the operation of government, apparently, *was* economists' business. And they got their big chance in war.

    Following the many roads by which economists entered the public arena, Bernstein finds that the profession came into its own through its impact on national decision-making during World War II. Ironically, "Not individualism but rather statism provided the special circumstances" for American economists to obtain prestige and power. (p. 89) "In point of fact, it was statism and centralized economic policy practice that had brought economists and their discipline to the prominence and influence they [came to] enjoy (p. 194)." The irony does not escape him: "It is one of the great ironies of this history that a discipline renowned for its systematic portrayals of the benefits of unfettered, competitive markets would first demonstrate its unique operability in the completely regulated and controlled economy of total war" (p. 89).

- Yet even when applying their theories and practices to the non-market environment of government, mainstream economists have relied insistently on the market model. Because mainstream economists in the U.S. and elsewhere have been so market-focused for so long, production outside the market has been erased from the equations of economics. As Albert and Hahnel observe (1990), for at least a century, "market mechanism" has been equated with "economic mechanism," which has resulted in the labeling of "nonmarket mechanisms" for the provision of public goods as "political" and, hence, noneconomic.

- So now, government is considered to have an economic role only (or primarily) in cases of "market failure." This logic de-legitimizes the value of public production in its own right. As Léon Walras told us a century ago, "The theory of exchange based on the proportionality of prices to intensities of the last wants satisfied... constitutes the very foundation of the whole edifice of economics" (cited in Ogle 2000). And, as Neva Goodwin has most recently concluded (2014a, pp. 100, 108), "the rigid neoclassical paradigm" has so long and so confidently presumed that the market itself could and would provide for the common good in most areas, that 20th century economists have "pursued the optimistic program of modeling a world in which perfect markets lead to optimum social outcomes."

- Granted this optimistic market logic, when and wherever government acts, it may stand accused of "intervening" in the economy. There is no viable and explanatory concept of an actual, let alone a legitimate, public non-market economy. So pervasive is the creed that government only "intervenes" in what is thought to be the valid, market economy that even literature from the Congressional Research Service (Labonte 2010) relegates government to an outsider role.

- The term "non-market" and its meaning remain elusive. For example, Karl Polanyi wrote extensively about the differences between markets and non-markets but did not deal with the dynamics and forces of production in the non-market public economy. Neither do such widely-cited economists of the public sector as Robert Dahl and Charles Lindblom. When Charles Wolf attempted to construct a theory of "non-market failure,"—meaning government failure—he used market-centric theory as his scaffolding. Kenneth Arrow considers market versus non-market "allocation" and tacitly acknowledges the social construction of public goods, but he holds faithfully to the creed that government actions represent "reactions of society to compensate for market failures." Even where an economist like Arnold Wentzel (2011) contends that "Market vs state is the wrong debate" and further acknowledges that "the state" is a part of the "non-market sector," he refrains from analyzing the distinct functions and processes of the public non-market.

- Joseph Stiglitz produced an entire textbook on "the economics of the public sector" (the latest edition in 2000) without recognizing the distinctive characteristics of a public non-market. Instead he relies on "market failure" to open a role for government. When he does discuss "government production," it is only to ponder when government should contract-out to private providers, given (he claims, without offering evidence) that there is a "compelling argument against public production: Often, governments seem to be inefficient producers." Usefully, he acknowledges that government production is more complex than market production and that in the public sector "choices are made collectively," but he is inconsistent and occasionally contradictory in his descriptions of collective choice, which in the end he "explains" mathematically with a graph of aggregated individual demand curves. Finally, he propagates the idea of a trade-off between private and public goods, failing to take into account empirical evidence of "crowding in"—the fact that some kinds of public investment in fact increase private investment. (Economist 2014b; Stretton and Orchard 1994, p. 73).

- Libertarian literature, studiously attentive to (the dangers of) government, does acknowledge non-market, public production if only to make the case that government does too much. A chapter on "The Economics of Collective Decision-Making" in a libertarian textbook announces that "it is crucially important to recognize that **government is simply an alternative form of economic organization**". It almost sounds Polanyi-ish. However, the text goes on to apply market-fundamentalist analysis to explain how government (allegedly) works. Similarly mired in market fundamentalism are the writings of Hal R. Varian (formerly an academic but now chief economist at Google), Tyler Cowen, James M. Buchanan (2003) and others who come from a libertarian or market-utopian perspective.

- Stretton and Orchard, in *Public Goods, Public Enterprise and Public Choice* (1994), provide an excellent critique of neoclassical economics and public choice theory (discussed below). They also brilliantly explain and defend the role of government. Sadly, they fall short of understanding the distinctiveness of the public non-market economy. In their view (p. 185), there are

three modes of production: public enterprise, private enterprise and unpaid work in households and voluntary associations. They have different characteristics [never detailed] and need different relations with government. Public policies affect their efficiency, their shares of capital resources and their roles in the economy as a whole. Policymakers should keep all three in mind. But that is not encouraged by prevailing theoretical models— however else they differ, neoclassical and marxist and postkeynesian models are all models of a single capitalist mode of production with varying amounts of market failure and government intervention.

Remarkably, even *they* adopt the mainstream rhetoric about government "intervention." And, oddly, in this passage government is held outside of the three modes of production.

Elsewhere in their book they do discuss government as a producer, but still they fail to construct a theory or offer an explanation of public non-market production. Instead they blur market and non-market production by the government, using two categories: "public enterprises" and "government" (p. 195). For them, public enterprises may operate under market conditions or may not (p. 205). In this construction, public enterprises supply goods and services that are free, such as education, libraries, census and statistical services, legal records and all types of public infrastructure, as well as providing goods and services at market prices. "Government" in their construction provides things like law and order, regulation of working conditions, trade policies, industrial safety, waste disposal, commercial and consumer credit. Since they blur market and non-market, it is not clear why a particular good or service falls into one category or the other; they offer no definition or classification scheme.

- Mainstream collective action theory is of no use for understanding non-market production. Stretton and Orchard (1994) capture some of the flaws of standard collective action theory: "A common theme is that the provision of public goods allows so much freeloading and self-interested contrivance by powerful groups and individuals that societies do well to make do with as few taxes and public goods as possible. An influential leader of that school of thought is Mancur Olson …The curious argument of The Logic of Collective Action [Olson's major work] is this: because freeloaders can gain more from collective action than the collective actors can, collective action is never rational." (pp. 66–67). David Bollier (2013) is also informative about collective action. In an article on Olson's Logic of Collective Action, he quotes Jonathan Rauch of the Brookings Institution saying that the book

  …blew a hole in the hull of American political science's leading postwar theory, pluralism, which saw transactional interest-group politics as basically fair and functional so long as everyone was at the bargaining table. Wrong, said public choice: the table is tilted. Unusually, the public-choice analysis found support from both ends of the political spectrum. Liberals embraced the idea that the system was biased toward the concentrated power of corporations; conservatives embraced the idea that political decision making is inherently unfair. Down went pluralism.

- "Public economics" was the topic of a conference in 1968 sponsored by the International Economics Association in collaboration with the French Centre National de la Recherche Scientifique. The presentations were gathered into a volume: *Public Economics; An Analysis of Public Production and Consumption and their Relations to the Private Sectors* (Margolis and Guitton 1969). The papers covered a range of topics, from pricing and investment in public enterprises, to application of economics analyses to the public sector, to public administration in public enterprises. They include Samuelson's presentation of his public goods theory and Musgrave's presentation on social goods. Still, none deal with the forces, dynamics and drivers within the public non-market system. In fact, J. Margolis, one of the book's editors, writing in the Introduction admitted that "government is a set of politically organized administrative units and therefore market concepts are insufficient to analyse fully government behavior," though he also contended that "the tools and concepts derived from the study of market behavior can play a useful role" (p. xiv). Still, he acknowledges that "The government is a very complex organization, and before we assert rules for its adoption we must know far more about the possibilities of its internal management and responsiveness to external influences." He concludes that "we require a body of theory comparable to the organization analysis for the private firm and market analysis for industries ..." and that while conference participants "grappled with these problems ...the primitive state of our theory is too apparent" (p. xxii).

More than forty years later there appeared another volume on public economics: *Studies in the History of Public Economics*, edited by Gilbert Faccarello and Richard Sturn (2012). The book's chapters had previously been published in *The European Journal of the History of Economic Thought* (Faccarello and Sturn 2010). Again, we find a range of topics covered, yet no contributor addresses the fundamental nature, scope and dynamics of the public non-market system. However, an insightful contribution by Madra and Adaman (2010) sheds light on the domination of public economics by the "public choice" school, starting with Anglophone countries, but spreading widely beyond. In addition, these authors call attention to the impact of this development on public goods and services themselves. Here is the summary of their premise:

Since the 1980s, neoliberalism has been replacing social democracy as the dominant platform for economic and social policy in all capitalist social formations. We understand neoliberalism not simply as the extension of the rule of the market and the limitation of the state, but rather as a radical reconfiguration of the relationship between the state and the market...[N]eoliberalism aims to transform the state and its mode of exercising sovereignty by modelling it on the logic of 'economic incentives'.

Public economics, the field of economics that studies the relationship between the state and the market, has been profoundly affected by this political, economic and cultural transformation. Nevertheless, we should equally acknowledge that theoretical developments endogenous to the discipline of economics have caused important changes in the core theoretical propositions and policy prescriptions of public economics. Moreover, these shifts and dislocations have, in turn, contributed to the rise of neoliberalism by performatively enacting an economisation of the language of institutional governance and reform in a wide range of social sites such as healthcare, education, defence, research and development, security, cultural production.

Madra and Adaman summarize their argument as focusing on emerging areas of theoretical concern that

have been crucial in shaping the development of public economics [including]: the increasingly systematic use of the assumption of opportunism (read as manipulability) in public economics when modeling all social behaviour, including those of bureaucrats [and] the growing recognition in social choice theory of the irreducible normativity of choice among various methods to aggregate exogenously determined individual preferences into social choice functions...

In short, the "public choice" school had come to predominate the field of "public economics".

- Useful definitions of non-market, relating specifically to public production, are those used by the OECD and in the National Income and Product Accounts (NIPA) in the United States.

From the OECD Purchasing Power Parity Methodological Manual (2006):

> The collective and individual services that government produces itself are referred to as
> "non-market services." This is because they are supplied free or sold at prices that are not
> economically significant.

From NIPA[1]:

> Nonmarket output consists of goods and of individual or collective services that are pro-
> duced by nonprofit institutions and by government and are supplied for free or at prices that
> are not economically significant. Individual services, such as education and health services,
> are provided at below-market prices as a matter of social or economic policy. Collective
> services, such as maintenance of law and order and protection of the environment, are
> provided for the benefit of the public as a whole and are financed out of funds other than
> receipts from sales. The values of the nonmarket output of nonprofits and of government
> are estimated based on the costs of production.

- To the extent that a connection has been drawn between economics and the
  public sector within mainstream economics, attention seems to gravitate to the
  issue of distribution (for example, Arthur Okun's notion of an
  "equality-efficiency" tradeoff) rather than the matter of production. There is
  much written about the absence of price in non-markets—as a defect—but little
  about what this means for production and for results measurement. Likewise,
  much is written about "value" and "public value", but not of relevance for
  explaining the dynamics and forces of the public non-market economy and
  production within it.
- One economist who did address public, non-market production was Paul
  Studenski, whose paper on "Government as Producer" (1939) is enormously
  useful. I summarized the major points in Chap. 5.

It is telling that nothing else so useful has appeared in the last seventy-five years.

Public Choice

As I began my research, I was advised by economists—traditional and pluralist—to
look at "public choice" theory. That was where I would find a "public economics." I
hadn't heard of public choice in the economics courses I had taken in the 1970s at
California State University East Bay or in the 1980s at Harvard and MIT, presumably because the "theory" was still in its infancy and had not yet permeated
university classrooms.[2] As I began to read, I was dumbfounded. The entire school

---

[1]Concepts and Methods of the U.S. National Income and Product Accounts (Chaps. 1–9) Nov.
2011; Bureau of Economic Analysis, U.S. Department of Commerce, NIPA Handbook (2011)
Chap. 2: Fundamental Concepts.
[2]According to Backhouse, an economic historian, public choice theory gathered steam beginning
in the late 1990s.

of thought is based on a market-centered view of the public economy. And it was determinedly anti-public.

In "The Rise of Free Market Economics: Economists and the Role of the State since 1970" (2005) Roger E. Backhouse outlines the development of the public choice school. It stems from a cluster of works published in the 1950s and 1960s by James Buchanan, Gordon Tullock, Mancur Olson, and Anthony Downs. It became a school, and a movement, when James Buchanan and Warren Nutter found a home for their efforts at George Mason University. In the mid-1980s George Mason opened the Center for the Study of Market Processes, with its largest supporter being the Koch Family Foundations.

Until his death in 2013, James M. Buchanan had been the leading proponent of public choice theory. A *New York Times* obituary noted that his beliefs "shaped a generation of conservative thinking about deficits, taxes and the size of government." Buchanan did not conceive of the theory, which arose obscurely through the economics literature of the late 1940s and 1950s, but

> from the 1950s onward, he became its leading proponent, spearheading a group of econ-omists [at George Mason University] in Virginia that sought to change the nature of the political process, to bring it more into line with what the group considered the wishes of most Americans...[and] argued for smaller government, lower deficits and fewer regula-tions. (McFadden 2013)

In a fascinating booklet on the history and background of public choice theory, Buchanan (2003) described how his book, *The Calculus of Consent,* written with Tullock in 1962, laid the groundwork for a movement they initially called **"Non-Market Decision Making**." But, as Buchanan explained,

> We were all unhappy with these awkward labels, but after several annual meetings there emerged the new name "public choice," for both the organization and the journal. In this way the Public Choice Society and the journal *Public Choice* came into being. Both have proved to be quite successful as institutional embodiments of the research program, and sister organizations and journals have since been set up in Europe and Asia (p. 5).

An advocate of public choice would characterize the field of economics as follows (per Stretton and Orchard):

> [E]conomics now has two branches: one explains how *market* goods are demanded and supplied and the other (public choice) explains how *public* goods are demanded and supplied."... In public choice economics "Government is a market-place where citizens trade taxes for public goods. Between citizens and politicians it is an exchange of support (votes, propaganda, campaign contributions) for benefits (p. 123).

A central tenet of public choice theory is that "politicians and (especially) bureaucrats seek to enrich themselves by enlarging their budgets." And they seek little else, as Tyler Cowen et al. (1994) argued in a paper: "Public officials often have little incentive to spend time and effort proposing policies that benefit others." This tenet has become so entrenched within public administration that a recent article on performance measurement in the *Public Administration Review* (Rabovsky 2014, p. 766) gives credence to "those who argue that public admin-istrators can generally be conceived of as self-interested, budget-maximizing bureaucrats who are constantly working to exploit their informational advantages in order to avoid meaningful oversight."

That so much evidence flies in the face of this and other tenets of public choice theory seems to have done nothing to halt its spread as a creed. In his book on *Bureaucracy*, James Q. Wilson (1989), no defender of government, provides numerous examples of federal agency leaders, including Melvin Laird, J. Edgar Hoover, and others, whose records disprove the claim that public servants are always motivated by self-aggrandizement. Wilson writes (pp. 179–81): "These examples and Tipermans's data offer very little support for the widespread notion that government agencies are imperialistic, always seeking to grow by taking on new functions and gobbling up their bureaucratic rivals. In particular the facts are inconsistent with the theory advanced by Gordon Tullock and William Niskanen (among others) that bureaucrats desire to maximize their agency's size." Yet Wilson himself by-and-large accepts the tenets of public choice theory.

Not only are politicians and government workers not to be trusted to act in the public interest. According to some public choice theorists, democracy itself can be shown to be invalid (in part, following Arrow's Impossibility Theorem). Buchanan (2003) himself protested such an extreme interpretation, yet he went on to explain that "Constitutional rules have as their central purpose the imposition of limits on the potential exercise of political authority." He elaborated: "in a constitutional democracy, persons owe loyalty to the constitution rather than to the government, as such, no matter how 'democratic' such decisions might be."

Public choice is not economic theory; it is political ideology hiding behind economic dogma. The case against it as both economic artifice and conservative promotion has been best made by Stretton and Orchard, who demonstrate the anti-government, anti-democratic stance of public choice theory. They suggest that public choice "reasoning seems to arise from the theorists' reluctance to 'come out' and identify themselves as open enemies of democracy or at least of universal suffrage…Governments are viewed as exploiters of the citizenry, rather than the means through which the citizenry secures for itself goods and services that can best be provided jointly or collectively."

Libertarians openly praise public choice theory, which they find fully compatible with conventional collective choice theory (as described above) and with the sweep of libertarian philosophy as anchored by the "Chicago," "Austrian," and "Virginia" schools of thought (Wandschneider 1994).

Stretton and Orchard (1994, p. 138) remind us that "Students are taught these images…of government. Such stuff educates rising numbers of the people we employ to govern us, and tells us not to hope or try to improve their quality. Insistently, explicitly, it tells *them* not to try to improve, except as 'legitimate thieves': to be anything else is irrational."

Public choice theory moved from academia into government decades ago. Reagan's Commission on Privatization issued a report that cited as validation for its recommendations on contracting-out the "problems of the American governing process identified by the public choice school" (Kettl 1993, p. 63). And Reagan appointed E.S. Savas, known as the "father of privatization," as Assistant Secretary of Housing and Urban Development (HUD). In 1983, Savas was forced to resign from his high position at HUD due to "abuse of office," chiefly for having HUD staff type, edit and proofread his book, *Privatizing the Public Sector: How to Shrink the Government*. Nevertheless, one reviewer (Reed 1983) gave the book high praise. Citing public choice theory as validation for Savas' privatization thesis, Reed tells us that "Privatizing is the peaceful way of dismantling the State brick by brick."

"When the medieval historian Richard Southern heard it said that there could never be much productive work or invention without competitive financial incentives," write Stretton and Orchard (1994), "he recalled that the eleventh and twelfth century revolutions in science, farm accounting and productivity were mostly conceived and carried out by celibates sworn to poverty" (p. 274). And they note that "Many public choice theorists now concede that as a description of political motivation and behavior the theory is false." So they ask (p. 126), "Why persist with assumptions which are neither true nor helpful to prediction?" and they are "driven to agree with [those] who believe that [the theory] continues partly as a source of dubious arguments for small government" (p. 133).

Public Administration Literature

In public administration literature, the closest in relevance to economics are debates about "public versus private management." Writings include: Paul Appleby's *Big Democracy* (1945), Herbert Simon's *Administrative Behavior* (1947, 1997), and Michael Murray's essay, "Comparing Public and Private Management" (1995). Simon offered interesting and possibly useful distinctions between market and non-market definitions of efficiency, and distinguished the process of administration (facts) from the purpose (values). Appleby, who came out of private business to work in FDR's administration, drew useful distinctions between private and public management. In contrast, Murray (with questionable premises and flawed analyses) concluded that there is no difference between the two. None of these (or other writers) have recognized the dynamics of non-market production, nor have they questioned the validity or utility of the market model for public, non-market service production.

"Public value" theory—a popular movement in some quarters of academia now— does not recognize the essential and fundamental differences between market and non-market production environments, and has been criticized as itself market-dependent (Dahl and Soss 2012, 2014).

A few scholars do attend to the differences between the "public" and "private" environments, stressing essential conceptual differences between "market" and "non-market." These include Ranson and Stewart in their various works in the 1990s including *Management in the Public Domain* (1994), and Hal G. Rainey and Young Han Chun's dissection of "public versus private management" (2007). An extensive treatment of "public/private distinctions" appears in Beryl Radin's

Federal Management Reform (2012). Yet none of these scholars delves into the nature of a public non-market environment.

Worse, they often set up a pointless, false dichotomy between "efficient" private sector, profit-driven management and public management based on other, and hence "inefficient," motivations. "The key substantive issue is whether there is an inherent conflict between the rational, private management model with its criteria of economic efficiency, and the political public management model with its criteria of consensus and compromise" (Michael A. Murray, cited by Radin 2012, p. 23). This dichotomy is not only false but misleading. For one thing, market organizations can be inefficient, and public, non-market organizations can be efficient. (See, e.g., my previous discussion of efficiency, "crowding-in" and "non-rival supply.") Moreover, public management is not about "consensus and compromise" any more than is private management. The real dichotomy is between organizations operating within market dynamics and driven by a goal of profit maximization, on the one hand, and on the other hand organizations operating within the dynamics of the public non-market and driven by collectively-determined public need.

Chapter 7
Developing an Intellectual Infrastructure

Ideas and concepts matter. Ideas frame theory; theory shapes concepts, and "Concepts," writes economist Meghnad Desai (2003), "influence how the world is viewed. They shape human expectations and actions." So does our phrasing of those ideas and concepts: Richard Musgrave observed in the 1960s that "Semantics, as the history of economic thought so well shows, is not a trivial matter" (Desmarais-Tremblay, p. 5).

A cogent and catalyzing concept of public economics is now called for. In her paper on the new economy, Neva Goodwin (2014b, p. 8) pointed up the urgent need to reconnect economic theory with the real world:

> the relationship between theory and reality is dramatically overdue to be realigned. In the 20th century, economic theory, regardless of its realism, was allowed to direct policies – some self-fulfilling, and some disastrously different from the announced intentions. We must move to a theory that is not only based on observed reality, but that also gives attention to what kind of economy is necessary, possible, and desirable.

Two decades ago, those in the world of public administration were unprepared to advance a vision of what was "possible and desirable." They were taken by surprise at the seizure of the reins of government by market-centric economics under the guise of Reinventing Government:

> those who study government and those who are practitioners of governmental management were understandably caught off guard by the sheer audacity of the entrepreneurial management advocates [Osborne and Gaebler] actively led by no less a personage than the Vice President of the United States (Moe and Gilmour 1995, p. 135).

Public administration theory has yet to catch up with what has been happening to governance. Likewise, economic theory. Neither discipline has addressed the conceptual vacuum that leaves practitioners of public administration stranded on a fantasy island of unrealizable marketized bliss.

To borrow from the concerns of the environmental movement (Keegan 2008): we need "to think our way out of [this] quandary, making clear that what is at stake is not another exercise in deconstructive frivolity." Stretton and Orchard (1994) stress the need for robust theory as "intellectual equipment" with which to counter the contemporary attack on government. Thomas O. McGarity (2013a, b) speaks of

© June A. Sekera 2016
J.A. Sekera, *The Public Economy in Crisis*,
SpringerBriefs in Economics, DOI 10.1007/978-3-319-40487-5_7

the need for a new "idea infrastructure" to rebuild devastated public capabilities. Luiz Carlos Bresser-Pereira (2014, p. 303) pleads for a serious dialog between economists and public managers.

It's high time. We need to lay the foundation for an economics of the public that:

- recognizes the legitimacy of the public economy, and not merely as a fill-in for "market failure";
- explains the distinctiveness and importance of non-market public production so incisively that the teaching of economics must change to accommodate this new understanding;
- informs a theory and practice of public administration that comports with democratic process and our constitutional framework for governance;
- helps restore government's capacity to operate effectively on behalf of all the polity;
- encourages and broadens participation in the electoral process.

Developing a new public economics must engage more than economists. As a truly cross-disciplinary endeavor, it requires collaborations among government administrators and leaders, and across such academic disciplines as public administration, sociology, economics, and political science. It must also investigate and adapt appropriate ideas and practices from business, taking care to ensure that those practices comport with public purpose and improve the day-to-day practice of *non-market* production. The effort must also make sense of how other democratic nation-states have been able to generate, educate and support a governmental production capacity that meets citizens' needs. Lastly, we should look to our own past for models of how government leadership overcame crises and how past leaders inspired effective democratic governance and managed effective public production.

Craig Calhoun, an American sociologist who would become director of the London School of Economics and Political Science in 2012, asked in 2004: "Can ideas of the public be reclaimed from trivialization by those who see all social issues in terms of an aggregation of private interests?" I should hope so. Toward that end, I conclude by highlighting some of the main themes that must be addressed in order to develop and promote a theory of the public non-market economy.

Defining Characteristics of the Public Non-market Economy

I have enumerated the characteristics of public goods supply in Chap. 5 on the Elements of Non-Market Production. None of these ideas is fully-developed. To be fleshed out or reshaped, each needs the collaboration of minds grounded in multiple disciplines. Topics to be developed include:

- Public purpose (meeting a public need as legislatively defined)
- Collective Choice (electorally manifested)
- Collective Payment (via taxes)
- Productive Flow (a three-node flow between three groups of agents)
- Unique input factors

  - votes as an input resource
  - authority to enforce as an asset

- Unique products
- Public goods re-definition
- Expenditures without spending
- No buyers
- Invisibility as a hallmark of effectiveness
- Non-rival supply
- Uncommon complexity of judging results.

Productivity of the Public (Advantages Inhering in Non-rival/Non-market Supply)

Standard economics holds, and political and popular opinion presumes, that the market is always superior to government in terms of productivity. Desirable forms of productivity and efficiency that are idiosyncratic to public non-rival, non-market supply go largely unrecognized. Here I list a few of them. They all require further conceptualization and development within a theory of the public non-market.

- **Crowding in**
  Public investment engenders increased private investment resulting in economic growth, higher than would have occurred without the public investment (as discussed earlier).
- **Non-rival supply**
  In non-rival, non-market production, agencies share information with other agencies doing similar work in order to multiply the benefits of lessons learned and to disseminate innovation. Before the onslaught of Reinventing Government and its ethos of competition, public agencies used to put significant effort into sharing "best practices" and "promising practices." That drive to share has been severely diminished in the era of public competitiveness and contracting-out of government. The challenge is to restore the norm of non-rival sharing in the public sector.
- **Single system efficiencies**
  For some goods and services, collective provision is more efficient than provision through competition; i.e., where heterogeneous, individual choice does not improve the provision and may in fact hinder it. Many fields of public activity

involve network and scale efficiencies. One example is the lower administrative cost per dollar disbursed of public, single-payer health care systems relative to the multitude of higher cost private health insurance schemes. Other examples: road networks and statistical data collection (Stone 2013).

- **Increasing returns to scale**
  Because it has the unique asset of the authority to enforce, government can produce increasing returns to scale through regulation of "commons." In her classic essay about the "comedy of the commons," Carol Rose (1986; summarized by Purdy 2011, p. 1035) reminds us that "the public trust began…as a way of ensuring that the channels of commerce, often literally waterways, were open to all, thus able to produce their ever-increasing returns to scale." And since increasing returns to scale are characteristic of certain types of products and services, which can become a source of monopoly power, some economists suggest that government should play a significant role in relation to such products.

- **Less risk-aversion, more innovation**
  Economist Mariana Mazzucato has produced an important body of research demonstrating the impressive innovativeness of government, particularly the U.S. federal government, with its historic propensity to make high-risk, high-payoff investments. Indeed, in *The Entrepreneurial State—Debunking Public versus Private Sector Myths*, Mazzucato (2013) proves that the public sector has consistently been more innovative than the private sector: "Not only has the government funded the riskiest research, whether applied or basic, but it has indeed been the course of the most radical, path-breaking types of innovation" (discussed in Littlefield 2014). Federal investments, for example, produced technological innovations that led to the Google search algorithms and the technologies behind the iPhone, not to mention the Internet itself (Mazzucato 2011; Upbin 2013).

- **Ability to harvest public investment for public benefit**
  Working with economist William Lazonick, Mazzucato (Lazonick and Mazzucato 2013) is also calling for "predistribution," wherein the public "risk-reward nexus" is reconfigured so that the risk-taker—the public through its basic science R&D investments—reaps some of the financial rewards of those investments, which are now accruing exclusively to private corporations who receive government grants. Predistribution is but one of several ideas for the better reaping of collective rewards from collective risk-taking.

Distinguishing Public from Private

One of the ongoing debates in public administration scholarship is whether "public" and "private" are different. The debate seems interminable. As more voices have joined the fray–some advancing an expanded notion of "governance"—the distinction has become ever murkier. This is dangerous, because the public interest invariably loses out when public and private purpose are conflated and confused.

This debate among public administration scholars, which took shape in the 1970s, originally concerned the question of whether public and private *management* are different. Some argued that management is a process so generic that its principles and techniques must be the same everywhere (Murray 1975). Others who researched the question remained unsure, while acknowledging that "public managers face greater challenges" (Rainey and Chun 2007/2009).

Currently a number of public administration scholars and "Public Value" theorists challenge the very distinction between public and private. A leading public value advocate, Barry Bozeman (1987), holds that "all organizations are public," and asserts (2007, p. 18) that "An organization is 'public' to the extent that it exerts or is constrained by political authority." Donald Kettl (2015) argues that it may no longer be possible to draw clear boundaries between government and non-governmental entities, given the complex "interweaving" of "power, functions, and responsibilities" between the two spheres.

The debate is more than academic. Besides having tremendous implications for public policy making and legislation, it is a fundamental question confronting the judicial system. Courts are now making decisions about constitutional claims based on their own attempts to deduce whether the interests of "state actors" and "private actors" differ, and have found that "private corporations…can effectively become 'public'" (Malatesta and Carboni 2015).

It is troubling that this debate goes on, especially if it resolves with the conclusion that there is no difference. However murky the analysis may be from an institutional perspective, the differences can be made abundantly clear from an economics perspective. It is time to put an end to this sterile discussion. In fact, as I have endeavored to show, there are intrinsic differences between public and private. A valid, coherent theory of the public economy could settle the debate.

Measuring Public Purpose

"It is not possible to evaluate the efficiency or performance of an organization without an understanding of its purposes." So say Ranson and Stewart (1994, p. 34), and they are exactly right. But for the last three decades, public sector performance management systems have been drawn from the template of the market, with implicit—and sometimes outright—acceptance of market values. These systems repeatedly fail to deliver what's needed in the public non-market.

Part of the problem has been the focus on "accountability," a buzzword under whose aegis have been smuggled in measurement systems designed from the start to "prove" that government doesn't work or works with gross inefficiency. Even when sincere attempts are made to improve "accountability," what is overlooked is that, in the public domain, accountability is at the ballot box. To be sure, in a democracy, citizens must hold government accountable for its actions; however, for accountability to work, you need an informed citizenry. How many decades has it been since government effectively communicated to ordinary people what it does for them on a daily basis?

In Chap. 5, I summarized the goals of a public non-market performance measurement system:

- to determine if you're doing the right thing (i.e., determining if you are achieving what the legislation was meant to accomplish);
- to determine if you're doing the thing right (and in order to improve how you do it);
- to inform legislators and citizens.

With these goals in mind, a public non-market performance measurement system must:

- Connect to legislative purpose
- Recognize the multiple constituencies of the public non-market
- Determine how to measure invisibility as effectiveness
- Determine how to measure the creation of positive externalities (short-, medium- and long-term)
- Establish modes of performance service adjustment
- Distinguish process from products
- Be part of an ongoing process of performance management that engages the public employees whose work and intellect produce public products and services.

Doing all this is difficult, but it has to be done if we are to get serious about performance measurement.[1] There is not space here to delve into my detailed recommendations on these topics. I would just add the following observations.

Goals, objectives, indicators, outputs, outcomes, impacts

The quest to improve performance measurement should be pursued within the context of judging results in the public non-market overall. In the arcane world of performance assessment, there are tremendous differences between concepts like "goals", "objectives", "indicators," "outputs," "outcomes," and "impacts." Tools for judging results may not even be comparable as one moves from performance measurement to program evaluation, or to comparison group studies, or to "experimental design with random assignment." And of course there are the dubious calculations of cost-benefit analysis.

---

[1]Federal performance management systems continue to falter (Clark 2012, 2014; Moynihan and Lavertu 2012). Many organizations are talking about or working to improve performance measurement. One is the Volcker Alliance, created by Paul Volcker in 2013 and, until recently, headed by Shelly Metzenbaum, former Director of Performance Management at OMB. Sadly, they too have not seen the need to shift into a new, public non-market perspective.

In the world of business, measuring results is, at bottom, stupendously simple: profits enable you to survive; net losses eventually put you belly up. Yet businesses can draw on vast resources—from university business schools and the enormous business consultancy industry—to help them contrive the best methods of assessing results. The public manager has nothing of the sort. To be sure, there is an enormous, and rapidly growing, performance measurement industry, with many for-profit vendors competing to sell their skills and wares to besieged public managers. Nowhere do we find cogent, comprehensive thought about the public non-market that would enable us to think big so that we can also think smaller—about techniques, tools, approaches and systems to logically and usefully measure public purpose.

Reviewing a book on "rethinking public administration" by Richard Clay Wilson (2013), a former City Manager of Santa Cruz (CA), Mary Hamilton (2014) sums up the problem:

> Wilson laments that private sector executives and managers get a lot of support from the academic discipline of business administration while government career executives and managers get very little from the discipline of public administration. According to Wilson, private sector leaders and managers have the benefit of studying with professors who are "interested in what works—they study performance and outcomes. They develop theories too, but they are outcome-oriented theories, not intellectual abstractions." As a result, private sector managers can draw on a robust literature that includes keys to success and reasons for failure. Unlike public sector leaders and managers, private sector leaders and managers are familiar with and use the academic literature in their field, thanks to publications like *Harvard Business Review*, which has no counterpart in public administration

Public administrators and workers are continuously confronted with demands to set goals and measure results. Sometimes these demands come from those who are well-meaning and thoughtful. But often they come from irresponsible or cynical market-centric ideologues whose ulterior motives should be challenged with the admonishment attributed to John Dewey (French 1998, p. 351) that "persons who continuously glorify goals without attending to the means of their realization are guilty of either insanity or insincerity."

Conclusion

Many people recognize that the policies and rhetoric of neoclassical economics are devastating our country; few are working actively to formulate an alternative economic framework for the public economy. No less than the Governor of the Bank of England recently warned that "unchecked market fundamentalism can devour the social capital essential for the long-term dynamism of capitalism itself" (Cohen 2014). Robert Atkinson, head of the Information Technology and Innovation Foundation, is one who advocates "presenting the case for loosening the grip of 'neoclassical economists' on policy" (Lohr 2012).

But that grip is still very tight. Neoliberal ideology and market-centric economics continue to dominate intellectual discourse about the causes of and cures for an America "in decay" (Fukuyama 2014). Many current and recent prescriptions for improving government operations are anchored in the axiom of market superiority and the belief that only by mimicking business can public agencies improve performance.

A few examples:

- Yale law professor Peter Schuck, author of *Why Government Fails So Often, And How It Can Do Better* (2014), advocates the "moneyball" approach to government reform" (Leonhardt 2014). Heedless of the fact that government operates in a non-market, Results for America has mounted a project called "Moneyball for Government."
- "Pay-for-performance," despite its proven failures (and its tragic impacts, as with the Veterans Administration wait-time scandal) is being expanded.
- Congressman Mark Meadows (R; NC), who in January 2015 assumed the Chair of the Government Operations Subcommittee of the House Oversight and Government Reform Committee, wants to "find solutions to federal workforce problems" by treating federal employees like private sector workers, punishing poor performers while paying bonuses to "outstanding" workers (Katz 2015)— with no idea of how to define "outstanding" or any appreciation of the immense barriers to constructing a reliable, valid performance measurement system in a non-market.

There are those who argue that our societal and economic problems can be solved if we simply act together, forming civic networks and "public-private-partnerships" between government and business. This approach ignores the fact that such alliances implicitly require the presence and energies of a capable, functioning government to ensure social stability and administrative capacity.

Claus Offe (2014) is a forceful voice challenging those who advocate networked governance, or those (meanwhile) awaiting the "withdrawal of the state":

> Some… argue that state power should merely "get out of the way"…Upon closer inspection this argumentation is a mirror image of the neoliberal critique of the state. It does not celebrate the liberating power of market forces but of *civil* society and the communal remedies it supposedly harbours. Despite our dissatisfaction with the inadequacies of public policy, we should not forget that the democratic state and its powers to tax, spend and regulate remain the major instrument for sharing responsibility among members of society. This instrument must not be done away with in favor of either the market or civil society, but rather must be strengthened and supplemented.

Offe continues, arguing that with "'network governance,' 'multi-level governance,' multi-party coalition governments, or 'public-private partnerships,'", we encounter not only "the problem of establishing clear links between decisions, their authors and their outcomes." Worse, as the state withdraws, we see (Offe 2012, pp. 30–33) the retreat of governments from major areas of responsibility, followed reciprocally by the retreat of up to a third of the citizenry from virtually all forms of political participation – the democratic idea of responsible government, or governmental accountability, is in the process of evaporating.

Mike Konczal (2014) argues that we must change "how we view the notion of the public."

> For decades the state, professionalized bureaucracy, democratic control of public finance, and the public itself have been vilified, while incentive pay and volunteerism—exemplified by homeschooling, armed self-defense, the anti-vaccination movement, and other forms of civic abandonment—have been ascendant. But as history shows, these rearguard actions make a fragile line of defense against the state's imperfections, and the ills of corruption and illegitimacy they breed can be far worse than any problems such anti-public measures may hope to solve.

In our attempts to cope with the social, economic, educational, and political devastations caused by a compulsively selfish ethos of competition and a creed of market omnicompetence, we cannot turn away from government because it has been most under the gun. Otherwise we will be subject, as Juha Siltala warns us (2013, p. 486), to the perils of the "fragilization of the state," the "downsizing of public services, disarming of all democratically controlled institutions, and turning citizens into consumers... Fragilization of the state will soon make life unpredictable, mutual contracts broken, and private costs of security enormous."

The solution, rather, is good and able government. "[I]t has been frequently forgotten," writes Allan Rosenhaum (2014a, p. 10), "that strong and effective government... is the single most important, and the one indispensible, institution of any modern society."

If we have any hope of resolving enormous issues like inequality and climate change, we must first combat all those campaigning to incapacitate government. Even those now proclaiming that government is necessary for the functioning of business or essential to reining in the excesses of unfettered markets must first work to restore to government what has already been dismantled in the name of the market.

The public economy—and the people's enterprise that we call government—is in crisis in the United States and in other Western nations. To reprise James Galbraith, we are witnessing the collapse of the public governing capacity.

Contributing to this collapse is a "false belief that you can get what you want from government while tearing it down" [thus the economist Neva Goodwin (2014a)]. And many are the forces working actively to suppress all news of public sector achievements on behalf of the polity. In an op-ed on "Hating Good Government," Paul Krugman (2014a) detailed the substantial successes of the Obama administration that have been intentionally buried by opponents who reject "any role for government that serves the public interest." He asks, "Why this hatred of government in the public interest?"

Such hatred is a compound of political ideology, moneyed interests, and economic creed, as James Galbraith has shown. Because such anti-government animus is ordinarily cloaked in the nostrums of mainstream economic theories, it has been made to seem not only legitimate but virtuous.

Law and Williams (2014) of the Centre for Research on Socio-Cultural Change (CRESC) in Britain, talk about "government as experiment" and analyze the 35-year experiment that started in the 1980s, in which

> the assumption was that the economy would prosper if markets were allowed to work properly. The idea was that competition would deliver efficiency and better services. The problem is that thirty-five years on government is still blindly running the same experiment even when its results are catastrophic…[and] now *we are living in a state of non-learning* (p. 2).

Of course, rebutting the market model of government and replacing it with a new, valid model of the public non-market is an enormous undertaking, one that may feel to reformers like tilting at windmills. Or they may find the intrinsic complexity of the non-market so overwhelming as to be unhelpful as a guide to practical, purposeful change. The public non-market is far messier than the idealized market.

But democracy is also messy. And complicated. And slow. As Michael Ignatieff (2014) has written, authoritarian rule is by contrast simple, efficient, and fast. Simplicity and speed, however, are not necessarily virtues. Democracy and non-markets are complicated. But, writes Ignatieff, "The central questions now are whether the new authoritarians are stable and whether they are expansionist. Authoritarian oligarchies can make decisions rapidly, while democratic societies struggle to overcome opposition in the courts, a free press, and public opinion."

We don't hear public calls for dismantling democracy in the United States because it is slow or messy. Democracy is still—in the West—a strongly-held societal value.

In *The End of the Experiment?* (Bowman et al. 2014), scholars at CRESC argue that "a fundamental reframing of policy choices is necessary" but that "government is unable to question the overall framework, and continues to try to impose an abstract version of competition and market rather than exploring alternatives." (p. 129).

Self-government is relatively new in human history. Running an enormous public, non-market, complex, amalgamated organization like the federal government is even newer. It's time to leave the state of non-learning and enter the era of learning. It's time to develop the conceptual tools that we need in order to think differently. The survival of our nation-state depends on the public governing capacity resisting the gale forces of neoclassical economics.

Appendix A
Case Example Details and an Additional Case Example

Following are: first, a more detailed version of the "Free Market Farce" Case Example from Chap. 2, and second, an additional Case Example.

"A Free-Market Farce": Procurement Rules and the "Obamacare" Website Rollout

Market Maxims Efficiency and Competition

Behind the disastrous rollout of the "Obamacare" website in October 2013 is a story of government attempts at market mimicry going back several decades. It is a story about procurement—a boring topic, most think. But changes to federal procurement rules[1]—designed in the 1990s to incorporate the alleged virtues of market competition—have had daily impacts on millions of lives.

The story has been well summarized by Janine Wedel and Linda Keenan (2010):

> Under the rubric of "reinventing government" and deregulation, the Clinton administration transformed contracting rules with regard to oversight, competition, and transparency. Industry associations worked to make government purchasing faster for the agencies and "friendlier" for contractors.

> The industry-energized reforms removed many of the traditional competition and oversight mechanisms that had been in place for decades and provided the statutory basis for new kinds of mega-contracts, such as the "Multiple Award" Indefinite Delivery/Indefinite Quantity (IDIQ) system, under which an estimated 40 percent of all federal government contracts are now awarded in areas ranging from computer support to analysis of intelligence. Like the euphemisms of politicians obscuring their intentions, the language of these awards is telling: "contracts" that aren't really contracts; "competitions" without real competition; "task" orders that may sound like small potatoes but can net billions of dollars for the contractor.

---

[1] In a forerunner to the 1990s changes, market "solutions" as procurement policy goes back to the Reagan era with its implementation of the "A-76" procurement doctrine, which itself goes back to the Eisenhower era.

© June A. Sekera 2016
J.A. Sekera, *The Public Economy in Crisis*,
SpringerBriefs in Economics, DOI 10.1007/978-3-319-40487-5

The stated intention of the "reforms" was a streamlined procurement process that would reduce the time, costs, and bureaucracy incurred in separate purchases and make contracting more efficient. As a result, over the past decade and a half, small contracts often have been replaced by bigger, and frequently open-ended, multiyear, multimillion-, and even billion-dollar and potentially much more lucrative (IDIQ) contracts with a "limited pool of contractors"...

Legally, IDIQ contenders engage in "full and open competition." But IDIQ contracts are not traditional contracts; they are agreements to do business in the future, with the price and scope of work to be determined. "Competitions" for open-ended contracts preapprove contractors for almost indeterminate periods of time (five to ten years, for instance) and money ranging into billions. When so anointed, contractors' names appear on a list maintained by a government agency. That agency, and usually other agencies, can turn to the chosen contractors, who now possess what has been called a **"hunting license,"** to purchase everything from pens to services... The old system required publicly announcing– each solicitation for government work over $25,000 — and then allowing companies to compete for it... [Emphasis added]

[Now] the award of a mega contract takes place behind closed doors and constitutes a virtual revolution in government procurement. Under the old system, overseers could document the amount of the contract because the amount was, more or less, clear when the contract was awarded. Under the current system, services are contracted in the form of "task orders,"...Issuances of task orders occur on an *ad hoc* basis without prior announcement... IDIQ contracts help maintain the façade of government efficiency...

Fast forward to 2007 when CGI Federal, the main coordinating contractor on the *healthcare.gov* project won a task order contract. CGI was "included in a pool of pre-screened, approved contractors in 2007, during the George W. Bush administration, and only firms in that pool were later allowed to bid for the Affordable Care Act work." In 2006, the federal Centers for Medicare and Medicaid Services (CMS) had used "a procurement method that has become increasingly common over the past decade. The agency first awarded an umbrella contract to a group of firms, and those firms were then eligible to bid on future IT work. Experts say this saves the government time because it shortens the subsequent bid process." (Markon and Crites 2013).

In September 2011 CGI Federal won a $93 million contract in which it was responsible for orchestrating the work of the 55 contractors also selected to work on the Obamacare website.

Another article about the website rollout connects the debacle to the procurement process: "CGI Federal's winning bid [in 2011] stretched back to 2007, when it was one of 16 companies to get certified on a $4 billion "indefinite delivery, indefinite quantity" [IDIQ] contract for upgrading Medicare and Medicaid's systems. [The rules] allow agencies to issue task orders to pre-vetted companies without going through the full procurement process..." In a July 2013 earnings call well before the disastrous October roll-out, CGI Federal's CEO Michael Roach noted: "In the Federal Government business, we continue to see more extensions and ceiling increases on our existing work, while we further leverage our position on contract vehicles." Those 'contract vehicles.' amounting to $200 billion, Roach referred to as a **"hunting license"** [my emphasis] (DePillis 2013).

In the quest for efficiency in the "competitive" procurement process, review of bidders' qualifications had been eliminated at the point of issuing a "task order"—the actual contract for work to be done. Thus, federal staff involved at that point missed the very troubled past of CGI in government contracting, and in particular its subsidiary AMS. "[F]ederal officials were not required to examine [the] long-term track record, which included a highly publicized failure to automate retirement benefits for millions of federal workers" (Markon and Crites 2013).

The procurement revolution of the 1990s, within which the ACA website contracting took place, is defended by Steven Kelman, who, as the Administrator of the Office of Federal Procurement Policy from 1994 to 1997, led the changes and wrote about the revisions in *Unleashing Change: A Study of Organizational Renewal in Government*. Reviewing Kelman's book, Vernon Edwards reports that the stated objective of the reform was to "reduce bureaucracy in the procurement system," with a focus on eliminating an "excessive emphasis on following rules." But Edwards (2005, p. 2) contends that:

> The main problem was not the existence of rules, but that most contracting office managers and contracting officers did not know what the rules were, and still do not, and did not have the professional skills that they needed—such as competitive process design, price analysis, negotiation, and business problem solving—and still do not. Pressured by reformers to serve *customers* (who are always right), unequipped and unprepared to assist *clients* (who rely on professionals to decide what to do and to act on their behalf), forced by personnel reductions to take over clerical tasks, and demoralized by their reduction in status to administrative assistants to program personnel, too many contracting officers traded poor bureaucratic practices for poor but expeditious practices.

In sum, a process ostensibly designed to create market-like efficiencies and streamlined competition predictably backfired, subverting the public interest. The debacle of the ACA website rollout cannot be laid at the door of simple government incompetence, except insofar as those in charge at the top did not understand the predictable pitfalls of the procurement process they were using.

Embracing Risk: Public-Private Partnerships (P3's)

Marketized Values Risk-Taking to Attract "Innovative" Financing

"Risk-management"—a concept and method borrowed from the private sector—is an increasingly popular topic in the public sector, as public employees are pushed to become more "innovative" and to look for creative financing methods to fund agency work once supported by taxes. For example there is growing interest in "enterprise risk management" in the "business" of higher education, including public higher education (Lovett 2014; Association of Governing Boards 2009) And a fast-developing movement toward "embracing risk" in the public sector can be found in infrastructure funding. The Departments of Treasury and Transportation have launched a major undertaking to expand public-private-partnerships (PPPs or P3s) and increase innovative financing. An "infrastructure summit"—"Expanding Our Nation's Infrastructure Through Innovative Financing"—was held in late 2014. One of the conference's main objectives was to explore how "new revenue and risk sharing models [can] make PPPs more attractive to both investors and state and local governments".

A Treasury Department paper prepared for the "summit" is replete with neo-classical economics reasoning and lauds PPPs as a way to "bring private sector capital and management expertise to the challenges of modernizing and more efficiently managing... infrastructure assets." The report cites privately managed public infrastructure in the UK and elsewhere as a model, and frets that the municipal bond market in the US, unique to our country, "has discouraged [local] governments from seeking private equity financing" (US Department of Treasury 2014, p. 4).

The Treasury Department has issued a handbook on risk management, noting that Congress has called upon states to develop "risk-based transportation asset management plans."

Despite the hopeful policy push by the Obama administration, research on PPPs shows that risk is not always (or perhaps not usually) "shared", but rather is borne by the taxpayer. An article by a scholar who studies privatization (Dannin 2014) discusses the "new hot concept...[of] infrastructure privatization through embracing risk" and reports that "so far there is no evidence to show that the private sector has shared, minimized or even assumed any financial risk in these deals in which the profits are privatized and the costs socialized." Another article, by the Associate Editor at Thinking Highways North America (Salzman 2014), describes highway PPP bankruptcies, and reports that "taxpayers are left paying off billions in debt to bondholders who have received amazing returns on their money...[V]irtually all— if not all—of these private P3 toll operators go bankrupt within 15 years of what is usually a five-plus decade contract...There do not appear to be any American private toll firms still in operation under the same management 15 years after construction closed. The original toll firms seem consistently to have gone bankrupt or 'zeroed their assets' and walked away, leaving taxpayers a highway now needing repair and having to pay off the bonds and absorb the loans and the depreciation."

Appendix B
Would-Be Replacements for New Public Management (NPM)

Largely in reaction to the spread of New Public Management in the U.S. (where it was called "Reinventing Government"), the U.K., New Zealand, Australia and parts of Europe, new theories of public administration are being advanced by public administration scholars. The main theoretical contenders attempting to replace NPM seem to be:

- New Public Service
- Public Value theory
- New Public Governance.

Following are brief summaries of each and observations about the ways in which they fall short in addressing the problems caused by the marketizaiton of government.

New Public Service

In 2000, Robert and Janet Denhardt (2000, p. 557) criticized NPM's subordination of concerns "for democratic citizenship and the public interest," and later expressed alarm at the connection between NPM and public choice economics (2007, pp. 10–11). Their alternative was to promote "citizen discourse" in the public interest. Their book on New Public Service opens (p. 3) by announcing that "Government shouldn't be run like a business. It should be run like a democracy." Yet they make no effort to challenge the economic axioms behind NPM, and seem not to comprehend the faux-market nature of public administration as now practiced within the NPM rubric. And, rather than arguing for fully democratic governance, they argue for a process that is *like* a democracy—a process of civic participation that mimics "democratic values."

© June A. Sekera 2016
J.A. Sekera, *The Public Economy in Crisis*,
SpringerBriefs in Economics, DOI 10.1007/978-3-319-40487-5

Public Value theory

In the 1990s, a "Public Value" movement was launched by Mark Moore of Harvard's Kennedy School of Government, who has acknowledged (Moore 2014, p. 465) its framing in opposition to the Reinventing Government movement of Osborne and Gaebler. The Public Value approach has also been advanced by Barry Bozeman, a widely-cited scholar of public administration.

Despite its positioning as an alternative, if not an antidote, to the market-centrality of New Public Management/Reinventing Government, Public Value theory in many ways embraces market-mimicking values. Moore himself acknowledges that in developing public value theory he wanted to mirror the creation of private value in the market. He considered that "perhaps the most important private sector idea for public managers to embrace was the idea that they should earn their keep by *creating public value*." [Emphasis in original].

Public Value theory has been criticized by Australian scholars Rhodes and Wanna (2007, pp. 411, 412), as "premised on a fundamentally non-democratic notion …[and]…because [Moore] distrusts the formal electoral process, managers have to turn to other surrogate measures of endorsement—such as client satisfaction or feedback [or] willingness to co-produce…" Questioning why private sector business techniques have not been widely embraced across Australian government, Rhodes and Wanna argue: "It is not because public managers are ill-trained, stupid or venal, but because private sector techniques do not fit the context, can be neutered by both bureaucratic and political games, and are not subjected to the same accountability as public management."

An even stronger criticism of Public Value theory comes from two scholars at the Humphrey School at the University of Minnesota. In "Neoliberalism for the Common Good? Public Value Governance and the Downsizing of Democracy," Adam Dahl and Joe Soss (2012) clarify "how public value should be understood in relation to neoliberalism and democracy." They argue that the Public Value approach "at its worst…produces a new variant of neoliberal rationality, extending and strengthening the very project its champions seek to overturn." In its Public Value rendering, citizen participation itself "ceases to be a democratic process in which citizens exercise power and becomes instead an instrument for enhancing the legitimacy of governing managers."

Elaborating upon their critique, Feldman (2014) writes:

> Dahl and Soss point out that public value theorists have misdirected their fire. They have attacked the neoliberal agenda as an effort to shrink government, when, in fact, the real victory of the neoliberals has been to fuse government and the private sector, often to the disadvantage of the public, as evidenced by the capture by private contractors of so much of what had been the realm of civil servants. The "market template" that neoliberals use as foundation for that fusion has also been adopted as a model for public value, so public managers are encouraged to "pursue public value by cultivating an entrepreneurial and managerial imagination," while their "[l]eading works say almost nothing about the realities of entrenched power and political bias, the barriers to democratization, or what it would take to overcome them." (p. 504)

New Public Governance

The New Public Governance (NPG) is a "plural and pluralist" theory advanced in Europe more forcefully than in America. Its chief proponent is a British professor of public management, Stephen P. Osborne (presumably no relation to the American David Osborne), who takes into account the historical flux and contemporary fixations of public administration, which, in his view, has passed through "three dominant modes":

> – a longer, pre-eminent one of PA [Public Administration], from the late nineteenth century through to the late 1970s/early 1980s; a second mode, of the NPM, through to the start of the twenty-first century; and an emergent third one, of the NPG, since then. (Osborne 2006, p. 378).

It is striking that NPG theory asserts that the marketization of government through NPM has been "transitory." That is certainly not the case in the United States, where market values and precepts still very much reign and are daily becoming more entrenched. It appears that NPG proponents accept the transplantation of market values and goals onto the public sphere as a given, even as they object to the intrusion of such market practices as "Lean" production. Most problematically, NPG does not address the dismantling of the capabilities of government agencies as the state is hollowed out, nor does it discuss in any depth the threat to democracy posed by marketized public values.

Instead, NPG emphasizes cooperation between state and non-state actors to achieve policy objectives. There are, in brief, four key features of NPG:

1. The blurring of boundaries between state and non-state actors in tackling social and economic problems.
2. Regular collaboration between Government and other actors.
3. The pooling of communal, state, and other resources.
4. The autonomy of a network of actors independent of government.

Possibly the most eloquent, pointed and accurate analyst of the implications of this and other new governance movements is the political sociologist Claus Offe. He writes (2010, pp. 99–100):

> [W]e need to understand and appreciate that the promotion of civic responsibility and cooperation is (some might say paradoxically) largely a matter of *public policy*. It is not the *retreat* of the state that lets civil society flourish; it is rather the outcome of public policies which encourage and help develop... the willingness and ability of citizens to assume and share social responsibilities...Much of civil society exists today in a state of what one could call 'cognitive closure': a condition of ignorance, inattention, and affective distance to the needs and problems of others.

Such cognitive closure is now exacerbated by the fiscal starvation of government, in which the state "reduces the agenda of its previously taken-for-granted responsibilities and retreats to a minimalist agenda" (Offe 2012, p. 31). Offe also writes (2010) that "[*T*]*he chronic need of most governments [becomes] to unburden the state budget by replacing state-organized and state-financed programs and services by voluntary ones that are provided for by civil society actors*"…[Such] chronic symptoms of fiscal stress…can be seen as a continuation of privatization moves of the heydays of neo-liberalism, with the difference that this time it is not the market to which services are being devolved, but civil society and that responsibilities assigned to civil society actors (such as charitable foundations, corporations, associations, religious communities, and individual citizens) (pp. 93, 99)." …As the state withdraws, fully or in part, from funding services and entitlements, citizens are left with no choice but to comply and to take on responsibility for their present and future selves—to the extent, that is, that their incomes allow them to do so (Offe 2012, p. 32).

Offe (2014, p. 9) calls this the "responsibilization" of the citizen, which puts the onus on individual actors for what are, or should be, shared social responsibilities, which should be addressed through effective democratic governance. He argues that "constituted and democratically accountable state power should not be written off as an important approach to solving the problem of sharing social and environmental responsibilities. The democratic state, in spite of its limitations, remains—or must be restored to its role as—a key strategic agent both in containing the negative externalities of individual choice and creating and implementing collectively binding solutions.

References[2]

Afonso, António, Ludger Schuknecht, and Vito Tanzi (2006, January) Public sector efficiency: evidence for new EU member states and emerging markets. European Central Bank Working Paper Series No. 581, https://ideas.repec.org/p/ecb/ecbwps/20060581.html

Albert, Michael, and Robin Hahnel (1990) A quiet revolution in welfare economics. Princeton University, Princeton. https://zcomm.org/wp-content/uploads/zbooks/www/books/quiet.htm

Amadae, S M (2003) Rationalizing capitalist democracy: the Cold War origins of rational choice liberalism. University of Chicago, Chicago.

Amey, Scott H (2009, June 16) Project on Government Oversight, Testimony before the House Committee on Oversight and Government Reform, Subcommittee on Management, Organization, and Procurement.

Amey, Scott H (2012a, March 28) Bad Business: POGO's Scott Amey testimony on Contractors: how much are they costing the government? Project on Government Oversight

Amey, Scott H (2012b, March 29) Contractors: How much are they costing the government? Congressional Testimony: Ad Hoc Subcommittee on Contracting Oversight http://www.pogo.org/our-work/testimony/2012/co-gp-20120329-scott-amey-contractors-costing-government.html

Anechiarico, Frank (2007) The New Public Management at middle age: critiques of the performance movement. Public Admin. Rev. 67(4): 783–786. doi 10.1111/j.1540-6210.27.761.x

Appleby, Paul H (1945) Big democracy. Alfred A. Knopf, New York. https://archive.org/details/bigdemocracy029139mbp

Arrow, Kenneth (1963, December) Uncertainty and the welfare economics of medical care. Amer. Econ. Rev. 53(5): 941–973

Association of Governing Boards of Universities and Colleges, and United Educators (2009) The state of enterprise risk management at colleges and universities today. http://agb.org/reports/29/state-enterprise-risk-management-colleges-and-universities-today

Backhouse, Roger E (2002) The ordinary business of life: a history of economics from the ancient world to the twenty-first century. Princeton University, Princeton and Oxford

Backhouse, Roger E (2005) The rise of free market economics: economists and the role of the State since 1970. Hist. Polit. Econ. 37(Suppl 1): 355–392. doi:10.1215/00182702-37-Suppl_1-355

Backman, Karen Hedwig (2012, April 26) Postal Accountability and Enhancement Act of 26. Daily Kos. http://www.dailykos.com/story/2012/4/26/1086631/-Postal-Accountability-and-Enhancement-Act-of-2006

Baker, Bruce E and Pamela A Kelly (2008) A primer on BAE's government accounts. Bureau of Economic Analysis Survey of Current Business 88(3): 290–38. http://www.bea.gov/scb/toc/0308cont.htm

---

[2]Note: All online citations effective as of March 3, 2016, unless otherwise noted.

© June A. Sekera 2016
J.A. Sekera, *The Public Economy in Crisis*,
SpringerBriefs in Economics, DOI 10.1007/978-3-319-40487-5

Baker, Dean (2014, October 27, updated December 27) The ebola vaccine, traffic congestion and global warming. Huffpost Business. http://www.huffingtonpost.com/dean-baker/the-ebola-vaccine-traffic_b_6058318.html

Barro, Josh (2014, December 19) An economist goes Christmas shopping. New York Times, p. SR2 http://www.nytimes.com/2014/12/21/upshot/an-economist-goes-christmas-shopping.html

Batchelder, Lily, and Eric Toder (2010, April) Government spending undercover: spending programs administered by the IRS. Center for American Progress. https://www.americanprogress.org/issues/tax-reform/report/2010/04/13/7580/government-spending-undercover/

Bernstein, Michael A (2001) A perilous progress: economists and public purpose in twentieth-century America. Princeton University, Princeton

Bogart, Ernst L (1939) Government expansion in the economic sphere. Annals Amer. Acad. Polit. Soc. Sci. 206: 1–5

Bollier, David (2002) Silent theft: the private plunder of our common wealth. Routledge, New York.

Bollier, David (2013, March 7) The logic of collective action: the fall of an iconic theory? David Bollier [blog]: News and perspectives on the common. http://bollier.org/blog/logic-collective-action-fall-iconic-theory

Bowker, Geoffrey C, and Susan Leigh Star (1999) Sorting things out: classification and its consequences. MIT, Cambridge MA

Bowker, Geoffrey C, and Susan Leigh Star (2006) Sorting things out: classification and its consequences. Revised ed., MIT, Cambridge MA

Bowman, Andrew, Julie Froud, Sukhdev Johal, John Law, Adam Leaver, Mick Moran, and Karel Williams (2014) The end of the experiment? From competition to the foundational economy. Manchester University, Manchester; Palgrave Macmillan, New York

Box, Richard C (1999) Running government like a business: implications for public administration theory and practice. Amer. Rev. Public Admin. 29(1): 19–43. doi: 10.1177/02750749922064256

Bozeman, Barry (1987) All organizations are public: bridging public and private organizational theories. Jossey-Bass, San Francisco

Bozeman, Barry (2007) Public values and public interest: counterbalancing economic individualism. Georgetown University, Washington, D.C.

Braudel, Fernand, translated by Siân Reynolds (1981) Civilization and Capitalism, 15th-18th Century. Volume 1: The structures of everyday life: The limits of the possible. Collins, London; University of California Press, Berkeley

Brechin, Grey (2014, August 6) The fire sale of the Post Offices. Consortium News. https://consortiumnews.com/2014/08/06/the-fire-sale-of-the-post-offices/

Bresser-Pereira, Luiz Carlos (2014) Public managers and the economists. Public Admin. Rev. 74 (3): 303–304. doi: 10.1111/puar.12192

Bruni, Frank (2014, October 18) The virus of cynicism. New York Times, p SR3

Buchanan, James M (2003) Public choice: the origins and development of a research program. https://publicchoicesociety.org/content/general/PublicChoiceBooklet.pdf

Bureau of Economic Analysis, U.S. Department of Commerce (2011) NIPA handbook: concepts and methods of the U.S. national income and product accounts (December) Accessed November 2012.

Caldwell, Bruce (2005) Hayek's challenge: an intellectual biography of F. A. Hayek. University of Chicago, Chicago

Calhoun, Craig (2004) Toward a more public social science = Word from the President. In the President's Report. Social Science Research Council, pp 14–18.

Cappiello, Dina (2014, June 2) Senate to take up new VA bill to address scandal. Boston Globe. http://www.bostonglobe.com/news/nation/2014/06/01/senate-take-new-bill-address-scandal/10zgKRALRjo8ZwlaQ3LbhM/story.html

Carroll, Aaron E (2014a, July 28) The problem with 'pay for performance' in medicine. New York Times. The Upshot

Carroll, Aaron E (2014b, October 20) Bad news for Obamacare: pay-for-performance doesn't work. Forbes

Center for Media and Democracy (2015a) ALEC exposed: ALEC's legislative agenda on privatization. http://www.alecexposed.org/wiki/ALEC_%26_Privatization

Center for Media and Democracy (2015b, 9 March) Sourcewatch: Corrections Corporation of America. http://www.sourcewatch.org/index.php/Corrections_Corporation_of_America

Chassey, Paul, and Scott H. Amey (2011, September 13) Bad business: billions of taxpayer dollars wasted on hiring contractors. POGO Project on Government Oversight. http://www.pogo.org/our-work/reports/2011/co-gp-20110913.html

Chen, Michelle (2014, August 25) When workplace training programs actually hinder workers. The Nation. http://www.thenation.com/article/when-workplace-training-programs-actually-hinder-workers/

Chetty, Raj, John N. Friedman, and Jonah E. Rockoff (2014) Measuring the impacts of teachers II: Teacher value-added and student outcomes in adulthood, American Economic Rev.104(9): 2633–2679 10.1257/aer.104.9.2633

Chick, Victoria (2011, November 18) Economics is lost – it must rediscover life's values. The Guardian. http://www.theguardian.com/commentisfree/2011/nov/18/economics-keynes-schumacher

Chick, Victoria (2013) The future is open: on open-system theorising in economics. In: Jespersen, Jesper and Mogens Ove Madsen (eds) Keynes's economics today, vol II: Teaching post-Keynesian economics. Edward Elgar, Cheltenham, pp 56–72. doi: 10.4337/9781782547006.00009

Choudhury, Nusrat (2014, February 6) Court-sanctioned extortion by private probation companies: modern debtors' prisons. ACLU blog, concerning the Human Rights Watch report, Profiting from probation. https://www.aclu.org/blog/court-sanctioned-extortion-private-probation-companies-modern-debtors-prisons

Christensen, Tom, and Per Laegreid (eds) (2011) Ashgate research companion to New Public Management. Ashgate, Burlington and Farnham

Clark, Charles S (2012 October) Do performance reforms change how federal managers manage? Governance Studies, No. 52

Clark, Charles S. (2013) CFOs lament decline in government services. Gov Exec Oct. 8, 2013; http://www.govexec.com/management/2013/10/chief-financial-officers-lament-decline-government-services/71564/

Clark, Charles S (2014 September 29) Agencies lose ground in performance management, GAO finds. Gov Exec. http://www.govexec.com/management/2014/09/agencies-lose-ground-performance-management-gao-finds/95354/

Cohen, Roger (2014 May 29) Capitalism eating its children. New York Times. Opinion Pages

Collins, Neil (2012) Challenging New Public Management. Powerpoint, University College Cork, Ireland. http://www.slideserve.com/zeph-ruiz/challenging-new-public-management

Committee on Veterans Affairs, US Senate (2004), Report on proposed Department of Veteran Affairs Health Care Personnel Enhancement Act of 2004 (S2484). http://www.gpo.gov/fdsys/pkg/CRPT-108srpt357/pdf/CRPT-108srpt357.pdf .

Cornes, Richard, and Todd Sandler (1994) "Are public goods myths?" J. Theor. Polit. 6(3): 369–385. doi: 10.1177/0951692894006003006

Cowen, Tyler, Amihal Glazer, and Henry McMillan (1994) Rent seeking can promote the provision of public goods. Econ. and Polit. 6(2): 131–145. doi: 10.1111/j.1468-0343.1994.tb00092.x

Dahl, Adam, and Joe Soss (2012, June) Neoliberalism for the common good? Public Value governance and the downsizing of democracy. Paper for Creating Public Value conference, Humphrey School of Public Affairs, University of Minnesota

Dahl, Adam, and Joe Soss (2014) Neoliberalism for the common good? Public value governance and the downsizing of democracy. Public Admin. Rev. 74 (4): 496–504 doi: 10.1111/puar.12191

Dannin, Ellen (2014, October 16), "US Treasury and Transportation Departments hold a privatization party. Truthout. http://www.truth-out.org/news/item/26847-us-treasury-and-transportation-departments-hold-a-privatization-party

Davies, William (2014a) Limits of Neoliberalism: authority, sovereignty and competition. Sage, London and Thousand Oaks

Davies, William (2014b, May 19) How 'competitiveness' became one of the great unquestioned virtues of contemporary culture. London School of Economics and Political Science, British Politics and Policy blog. http://blogs.lse.ac.uk/politicsandpolicy/the-cult-of-competitiveness/

Denhardt, Robert B. and Janet Vinzant Denhardt (2000, November) The new public service: Serving rather than steering" Public Admin. Rev. 60 (6): 549–559

Denhardt, Janet V, and Robert B Denhardt (2007) The new public service: serving, not steering. M E Sharpe, Armonk and London

DePillis, Lydia (2013, October 16) Meet CGI Federal, the company behind the botched launch of HealthCare.gov. Washington Post. https://www.washingtonpost.com/news/wonk/wp/2013/10/16/meet-cgi-federal-the-company-behind-the-botched-launch-of-healthcare-gov/

Desai, Meghnad (2003) Public goods: a historical perspective. In: Kaul, Inge et al. (eds) Providing global public goods: managing globalization. Oxford University, Oxford, pp 63–77. doi:10.1093/0195157400.001.0001

Desmarais-Tremblay, Maxime (2013, May) On the definition of public goods: assessing Richard A. Musgrave's contribution. Paper presented at 17th Annual Conf Europ Soc Hist Econ Thought, Kingston University, London. Also available at Documents de travail du Centre d'Economie de la Sorbonne. https://halshs.archives-ouvertes.fr/halshs-00951577/document

Diefenbach, Thomas (2009) New public management in public sector organizations: the dark sides of managerialistic "enlightenment." Public Admin. 87(4): 892–909. doi: 10.1111/j.1467-9299.2009.01766.x

DiIulio, John J, Jr (2014) Bring back the bureaucrats. Templeton Press, West Conshohocken, PA

Dixon, Ruth, and Martin Lodge (eds) (2012) Explorations in governance: a collection of papers in honour of Christopher Hood. Institute for Government, London School of Economics

Domhoff, William G (2005, April) The four networks theory of power: a theoretical home for power structure research. http://www2.ucsc.edu/whorulesamerica/theory/four_networks.html

Doswell, Charles A, III, and Harold E Brooks (1998) Budget-cutting and the value of weather services. Weather and Forecasting 13(1): 206–212

Economist (2012, October 23) Is it irrational to vote? The Economist. http://www.economist.com/blogs/democracyinamerica/2012/10/presidential-election-0

Economist (2014a, January 25) California: the recovery. The Economist. http://www.economist.com/news/leaders/215955-california-has-won-breathing-space-under-jerry-brown-now-he-should-tackle-taxes-debt-and-red

Economist (2014b, October 4) Public investments in infrastructure do the most good at times like the present. The Economist. http://www.economist.com/news/finance-and-economics/21621801-public-investments-infrastructure-do-most-good-times

Economist (2014c, October 25) Executive pay; moneybags. Should CEOs really be paid less? [Review of Indispensable and other myths: why the CEO pay experiment failed and how to fix it, by Michael Dorff] The Economist. http://www.economist.com/news/business-books-quarterly/21627553-should-ceos-really-be-paid-less-moneybags

Eden, Maya, and Aart Kraay (2014. February) Crowding in and the returns to government investment in low-income countries. World Bank Working Paper 6781

Editorial Board, New York Times (2016, March 28) A modern system of debtor prisons

Edsall, Thomas B (2014, August 26) The expanding world of poverty capitalism. New York Times, Opinion Pages

Edwards, Vernon J (2005) [Review of Unleashing change: a study of organizational renewal in government, by Steven Kelman]. Brookings Institution, 2005]. www.wifcon.com/anal/Kelman4.doc

Egan, Timothy (2014, March 6) Jerry Brown's revenge. New York Times, Opinion Pages

Ellig, Jerry, Maurice McTigue, and Henry Wray (2011, September 8) Government performance and results: an evaluation of GPRA's first decade. ASPA Series in Public Administration and Public Policy. CRC, Taylor & Francis Group, Boca Raton, London, and New York

Ellis, Joseph J (2015) The quartet: orchestrating the second American Revolution 1783 – 1789. Knopf, New York

EUROSTAT-OECD (2012) Methodological manual on purchasing power parities (PPPs). Permanent url: www.oecd.org/std/ppp/manual and specific url: http://www.oecd.org/std/prices-ppp/eurostat-oecdmethodologicalmanualonpurchasingpowerparitiesppps.htm

Faccarello, Gilbert, and Richard Sturn (eds) (2010) Studies in the history of public economics. [Selected contributions from the conference on the History of Public Economics, Université Panthéon-Assas, Paris, 10-12 December 28]. The European Journal of the History of Economic Thought 17(4)

Faccarello, Gilbert and Richard Sturn (eds) (2012) Studies in the history of public economics. Routledge, London

Fahrenthold, David A (2014, May 30) Breaking points: where government falls apart; how the VA developed Its culture of coverups. Washington Post

Farlex (2011) Governance. American Heritage Dictionary of the English Language. 5th edn. Houghton Mifflin Harcourt, Boston. http://www.thefreedictionary.com/governance

Feldman, Daniel (2014, Jul.-Aug.)) Public value governance or real democracy? Public Admin. Rev. 74(4): 504–505. doi: 10.1111/puar.12250

Fountain, Jane E (2001) Paradoxes of public sector customer service. Governance: An Intl J of Policy and Admin. 14(1): 55–73. doi: 10.1111/0952-1895.00151

Fourcade, Marion, Etienne Ollion, and Yann Algan (2014) The superiority of economists. Max Planck Sciences Po Center on Coping with Instability in Market Societies; Discussion Paper No. 14/3. www.maxpo.eu/pub/maxpo_dp/maxpodp14-3.pdf

Frederickson, David G, and H George Frederickson (2006) Measuring the performance of the hollow state. Georgetown University, Washington, D.C.

French, Roderick S (1998) Dewey for administrators: notes for an esthetic of administration in a democratic society. The Centennial Rev 42(2): 333–352. http://www.jstor.org/stable/23740049

Frey, Bruno S, and Margit Osterloh (2012) Stop tying pay to performance. The evidence is overwhelming: it doesn't work. Harvard Business Rev. 90 (1-2) http://hbr.org/2012/01/tackling-business-problems/ar/1

Freyss, Siegrun Fox (2014, December 2) Paradigm shifts in public administration — Toward a competitive, market-driven public administration model. Public Admin. Times http://patimes.org/paradigm-shifts-public-administration-competitive-market-driven-public-administration-model/

Fukuyama, Francis (2014 Sept./Oct.) America in decay: the sources of political dysfunction. Foreign Affairs 93(5): 5–26. https://www.foreignaffairs.com/articles/united-states/2014-08-18/america-decay

Gaebler, Ted, and Alexandra Miller (2006) Practical public administration: a response to academic critique of the reinvention trilogy. Administrative Culture/Halduskultuur 7: 16–23. http://halduskultuur.eu/journal/index.php/HKAC/article/view/37

Galbraith, James K (2008) The predator state: how conservatives have abandoned the free market and why liberals should too. Free Press, New York

Galbraith, John Kenneth (1958) The affluent society. Houghton Mifflin, Boston

George, Susan (2015), Shadow sovereigns: how global corporations are seizing power. Polity, Cambridge and Malden, MA

Giblin, Paul (2014, November 16) VA didn't track vacant medical jobs until this year. Arizona Republic. http://www.azcentral.com/story/news/arizona/investigations/2014/11/16/veterans-affairs-vacant-medical-jobs/19153069/

Goldscheid, Rudolf (1925), "A sociological approach to problems of public finance." In: Musgrave, Richard A and Alan T Peacock (eds) Classics in the theory of public finance. Macmillan for the International Economic Association, London, 1958, p 202–213

Good Jobs First, http://www.goodjobsfirst.org/

Goodsell, Charles T (2014) The new case for bureaucracy. Sage/CQ, Los Angeles

Goodwin, Neva R (2005) The limitations of markets: background essay. Global Development and Environment Institute, Tufts University. http://ase.tufts.edu/gdae

Goodwin, Neva R (2014a) The human element in the new economics: a 60-year refresh for economic thinking and teaching. Real World Econ. Rev. Issue 68: 98-118. www.paecon.net/PAEReview/

Goodwin, Neva R (2014b) Prices and work in the new economy. Global Development and Environment Institute, Tufts University, Working Paper No. 14-01. http://ase.tufts.edu/gdae

Goodwin, Neva R, Jonathan Harris, Julie A Nelson, Brian Roach, and Mariano Torras (2014) Principles of economics in context. M E Sharpe, Armonk and London

Goodwin, Neva R, Julie A Nelson, and Jonathan Harris (2015) Macroeconomics in context, 2nd edn. M. E. Sharpe, Armonk http://www.ase.tufts.edu/gdae/publications/textbooks/macroeconomics.html

Gopnik, Adam (2013, March 1) The sequester's market utopians. The New Yorker. http://www.newyorker.com/news/daily-comment/the-sequesters-market-utopians

Government Accountability Office, GAO (2013a) Tax expenditures: IRS data available for evaluations are limited. Report to congressional requesters, GAO-13-479, April 2013, www.gao.gov/assets/660/654273.pdf

Government Accountability Office, GAO (2013b) VA health care - Actions needed to improve administration of the provider performance pay and award systems. GAO-13-536, July 24, 2013, publicly released August 23. http://www.gao.gov/products/GAO-13-536

Government Accountability Office, GAO (2014) Managing for results: agencies' trends in the use of performance information to make decisions. GAO-14-747, September 26, 2014.http://www.gao.gov/products/GAO-14-747

Government Technology (1995, June 30) Indianapolis mayor Stephen Goldsmith. Gov. Technol. http://www.govtech.com/magazines/gt/Indianapolis-Mayor-Stephen-Goldsmith.html

Graham, Stephen (2009) When infrastructures fail. In Graham, Stephen (ed) Disrupted cities: when infrastructures fail. Routledge, New York, p 1–26

Gutmann, Amy (1987) Democratic education. Princeton University, Princeton

Hacker, Jacob S and Paul Pierson (2016) American amnesia: how the war on government led us to forget what made America prosper. Simon & Schuster

Hackett, Ursula (2012) The power of invisibility [review of The submerged state: how invisible government politicies are undermining American democracy, by Suzanne Mettler]. Oxonian Rev. 18(2). www.oxonianreview.org/wp/the-power-of-invisibility/

Hall, Charles A S et al. (2001) The need to reintegrate the natural sciences with economics. BioScience 51(8): 663–71. doi:10.1641/0006-3568(2001)051[0663:TNTRTN]2.0.CO;2

Hall, Charles A S, and Kent A Klitgaard (2012) Energy and the wealth of nations: understanding the biophysical economy. Springer Science & Business Media

Hamilton, James A (2012, April 19) Current U.S. Postal Service financial woes caused by 2006 law passed by GOP-controlled Congress. Allvoices. Accessed April 9, 2014, as http://www.allvoices.com/contributed-news/11972626-current-us-postal-service-financial-woes-caused-by-2006-law-passed-by-gop-controlled-congress but no longer online.

Hamilton, Mary (2014, May 23) What if we believed in management in public organizations? Public Admin Times

Hartocollis, Anemona (2013, January 11) New York City ties doctors' income to quality of care. New York Times, p A1 New York print edition http://www.nytimes.com/2013/01/12/nyregion/new-york-city-hospitals-to-tie-doctors-performance-pay-to-quality-measures.html?hp

Head, Simon (2011, January 13) The grim threat to British universities. New York Review of Books

Heires, Gregory N (2014, March 11) Corporate fat cats become the nation's richest 'government employees' by leaching off taxpayers. Reader supported news. http://readersupportednews. org/pm-section/78-78/22525-corporate-fat-cats-become-the-nations-richest-government-employees-by-leaching-off-taxpayers, earlier version posted at http://www.thenewcrossroads. com/2014/03/10/corporate-fat-cats-become-the-nations-richest-government-employees-by-leaching-off-taxpayers/

Hernandez, Carla (2014, September 16) Obama's college-ratings plan. Higher Education Assessment. https://higheredassessment.wordpress.com/2014/09/

Hodgson, Geoffrey M (2013) From pleasure machines to moral communities: an evolutionary economics without Homo economicus. University of Chicago, Chicago

Hogan, Bill (2014, April) Under siege: predators target homes of older Americans. AARP Bulletin 55(3): 22–26. http://www.aarp.org/money/taxes/info-2014/tax-liens-target-homeowners.html

Hood, Christopher (2001) Public management, new. In: Smelser, Neil J and Paul B Baltes (eds) International encyclopedia of the social & behavioral sciences. Elsevier, Amsterdam and New York, pp 12553–12556. http://christopherhood.net/pdfs/npm_encyclopedia_entry.pdf

Howard, Philip (2014) The rule of nobody: saving America from dead laws and broken government. W W Norton, New York.

Ignatieff, Michael (2014, September 25) The new world disorder. New York Review of Books. Adapted from 50th annual Ditchley Foundation lecture. http://www.nybooks.com/articles/ 2014/09/25/new-world-disorder/

In the Public Interest (2012, September 12) Profiting from public dollars: how ALEC and its members promote privatization of government services and assets. http://www. inthepublicinterest.org/profiting-from-public-dollars-how-alec-and-its-members-promote-privatization-of-government-services-and-assets/

Jamiel, Douglas (2014, May 4) Deride and conquer: dismantling the USPS. Truthout. http://www. truth-out.org/news/item/23471-deride-and-conquer-dismantling-the-usps

Joint Committee on Taxation, Congress of the United States (2014 August 5) Estimates of federal tax expenditures for fiscal years 2014-2018, prepared for the House Committee on Ways and Means and the Senate Committee on Finance. JCX-97-14, submitted November 7, 2014. https://www.jct.gov/publications.html?func=startdown&id=4663

Jones, Owen (2013, November 13) Why do private-sector zealots choose to ignore the countless ways public money underpins daily life? Independent (UK). http://www.independent.co.uk/ voices/comment/why-do-private-sector-zealots-choose-to-ignore-the-countless-ways-public-money-underpins-daily-life-8937628.html

Joyce, Phillip (2014, July 16) When performance measurement goes wrong in government. Governing. http://www.governing.com/columns/smart-mgmt/col-performance-measurement-scandals-lessons.html

Kalambokidis, Laura (2014) Creating public value with tax and spending policies: the view from public economics. Public Admin. Rev. 74(4): 519–526. doi: 10.1111/puar.12162

Kamarck, Elaine (2013) Lessons for the future of government reform; testimony before the House Committee on Oversight and Government Reform, June 18, 2013. Brookings Institution. http:// www.brookings.edu/research/testimony/2013/06/18-reinventing-government-future-reform-kamarck

Kamarck, Elaine (2016), online biography as Adjunct Lecturer in Public Policy, Harvard Kennedy School, John F. Kennedy School of Government, Cambridge, MA. https://www.hks.harvard. edu/about/faculty-staff-directory/elaine-kamarck

Kasdan, David Oliver (2012) "Great Books" of public administration, 1990-2010: revisiting Sherwood's survey in the wake of "Reinventing Government." Admin. & Soc. 44(5): 625–639. doi: 10.1177/0095399712455264

Katz, Eric (2015, January 13) Expect a carrot-and-stick approach from new workforce watchdog. Gov. Exec. http://www.govexec.com/oversight/2015/01/expect-carrot-and-stick-approach-new-workforce-watchdog/102777/

Keegan, Bridget (2008, Winter) [Review of Ecology without nature: rethinking environmental aesthetics, by Timothy Morton]. Studies in Romanticism 47(4): 581–584. http://www.jstor.org/stable/25602170

Kettl, Donald F (1993) Sharing power – public governance and private markets. Brookings Institution, Washington, DC

Kettl, Donald F (2015, Mar./Apr.) The job of government: interweaving public functions and private hands. Public Admin. Rev. 75(2): 219–229. doi: 10.1111/puar.12336

Kohn, Alfie (1986) No contest: the case against competition. Why we lose in our race to win. Houghton-Mifflin, Boston

Konczal, Mike (2014, November 10) Selling fast: public goods, profits, and state legitimacy. Boston Rev. https://bostonreview.net/books-ideas/mike-konczal-profits-state-legitimacy-parrillo-goldstein-balko

Krugman, Paul (2014a, January 18) Hating good government. New York Times, p A19 New York print edition. http://www.nytimes.com/2015/01/19/opinion/paul-krugman-hating-good-government.html?

Krugman, Paul (2014b, June 26) The incompetence dogma – So much for Obamacare not working. New York Times, p A29 New York print edition. http://www.nytimes.com/2014/06/27/opinion/paul-krugman-so-much-for-obamacare-not-working.html

Krugman, Paul (2014c, July 24) Left coast rising. New York Times, p A27 New York print edition. http://www.nytimes.com/2014/07/25/opinion/paul-krugman-california-tax-left-coast-rising.html

Krugman, Paul, and Robin Wells (2009) Microeconomics. 2nd edn. W H Freeman, New York

Labonte, Marc (2010, June 14) Size and role of government: economic issues. Congressional Research Service Report, 7–57

Lagace, Martha (2003, April 14) Pay-for-performance doesn't always pay off [on research of Michael Beer]. Harvard Business School, Working Knowledge site http://hbswk.hbs.edu/item/pay-for-performance-doesnt-always-pay-off

Law, John, and Karel Williams (2014, January) A state of unlearning? Government as experiment. Centre for Research on Socio-Cultural Change (CRESC) Working Paper 134. www.cresc.ac.uk/medialibrary/workingpapers/wp134.pdf

Lazonick, William, and Mariana Mazzucato (2013) The risk-reward nexus in the innovation-inequality relationship: who takes the risks? who gets the rewards? Ind. Corp. Change 22(4): 1093–1128. doi: 10.1093/icc/dtt019. www.policy-network.net/uploads/media/154/8167.pdf

Leonhardt, David (2014, July 15) The quiet movement to make government fail less often. New York Times, pA3. http://www.nytimes.com/2014/07/15/upshot/the-quiet-movement-to-make-government-fail-less-often.html

Light, Paul C (2003, September 5) Fact sheet on the new true size of government. Center for Public Service, The Brookings Institution. http://www.brookings.edu/research/articles/2003/09/05politics-light

Light, Paul C (2006, August) The new true size of government. New York University, Organizational Performance Initiative, Research Brief No. 2

Lind, Michael (2012) Land of promise; an economic history of the United States. HarperCollins, New York

Lipsky, Michael (2014) Assessing government performance through the lens of public sector workers [Review of The new case for bureaucracy by Charles T Goodsell]. Public Admin Rev 74(6): 806–07. doi: 10.1111/puar.12298

Littlefield, Ron (2014, October 22) Why Steve Jobs might have failed at government innovation. Governing. http://www.governing.com/cityaccelerator/blog/why-steve-jobs-might-have-failed-at-government-innovation.html

Lohr, Steve (2012, October 6) The seeds that federal money can plant. New York Times, p BU3 http://www.nytimes.com/2012/10/07/technology/making-the-case-for-a-government-hand-in-research.html

Lovett, Kenyatta (2014, October 14) Valuing risk as a new strategy for public higher education. Public Admin. Times. http://patimes.org/valuing-risk-strategy-public-higher-education/

Lowery, George (2001, Spring) From Maxwell perspective … putting the purpose in P.A. Maxwell Perspective, Maxwell School, Syracuse University. http://www.maxwell.syr.edu/news.aspx?id=227

Lowrey, Annie (2013, March 17) Tax credits or spending? Labels, but in Congress, fighting words. New York Times, p A1 New York print edition. http://www.nytimes.com/2013/03/18/business/economy/taxes-or-spending-budget-fight-in-congress-focuses-on-a-distinction.html

Lunney, Kellie (2014, November 6) VA Secretary says he's moving as fast as possible to remove bad apples. Gov. Exec. http://www.govexec.com/management/2014/11/va-secretary-says-hes-moving-fast-possible-remove-bad-apples/98372/

Luntz, Frank (2014, November 5) The midterms were not a Republican revolution. New York Times, pA31 New York print edition. http://www.nytimes.com/2014/11/06/opinion/the-midterms-were-not-a-republican-revolution.html

Lutton, Jonathan (2014, August 27) When agency websites outshine Amazon and Apple. Federal Computer Week (=FCW). https://fcw.com/articles/2014/08/27/snapshot-egov-satisfaction.aspx

Lynn, Laurence E, Jr. (2001) The myth of the bureaucratic paradigm: what traditional public administration really stood for. Public Admin. Rev. 61(2): 144–160 doi: 10.1111/0033-3352.00016

Mackie, Gerry (2011) Deliberation, but voting too, in Approaching deliberative democracy: Theory and practice, Robert Cavalier, Ed. pp 75–99.

Madra, Jahya M & Fikret Adaman (2010) Public economics after neoliberalism: a theoretical–historical perspective, The European Journal of the History of Economic Thought, 17:4, 1079–1106, DOI: 10.1080/09672567.2010.482997

Malatesta, Deanna, and Julia L. Carboni (2015) The public-private distinction: insights for public administration from the state action doctrine. Public Admin Rev 75(1): 63–74. doi: 10.1111/puar.12272

Mandl, Ulrike, Adriaan Dierx, Fabienne Ilzkovitz, European Commission (2008) The effectiveness and efficiency of public spending. Economic Papers 301. doi: 10.2765/25272http://ec.europa.eu/economy_finance/publications/publication_summary11904_en.htm

Margetts, Helen, Perri 6, and Christopher Hood (eds) (2010) Paradoxes of modernization: unintended consequences of public policy reform. Oxford University, Oxford

Margolis, J and H Guitton (1969) Public economics; an analysis of public production and consumption and their relations to the private sectors. Macmillan, London

Markon, Jerry, and Alice Crites (2013, December 22) HealthCare.gov contract: politics not a factor, but neither were firm's ties to failed projects. Washington Post.

Markkula Center for Applied Ethics, Santa Clara University (2014, June 10) Veterans Affairs: performance-based pay and the law of unintended consequences. Business ethics in the news. https://www.scu.edu/ethics/ethics-resources/ethics-blogs Accessed April 19, 2015.

Marr, Chuck, Chye-Ching Huang, and Joel Friedman (2013, February 28) Tax expenditure reform: an essential ingredient of needed deficit reduction. Center on Budget and Policy Priorities. http://www.cbpp.org/research/tax-expenditure-reform-an-essential-ingredient-of-needed-deficit-reduction

Mazzucato, Mariana (2011) The entrepreneurial state. Demos, London

Mazzucato, Mariana (2013) The entrepreneurial state–debunking public vs. private sector myths. Anthem, London and New York

McFadden, Robert D (2013, January 9) James M. Buchanan, Economic scholar and Nobel laureate, dies at 93. The New York Times. Obituary pages.

McGarity, Thomas O (2013a) Freedom to harm: the lasting legacy of the laissez-faire revival. Yale University, New Haven

McGarity, Thomas O (2013b, December 8) What Obama left out of his inequality speech: regulation. New York Times, Opinion pages http://opinionator.blogs.nytimes.com/2013/12/08/what-obama-left-out-of-his-inequality-speech-regulation/

Mettler, Suzanne (2010) Reconstituting the submerged State: the challenges of social policy reform in the Obama Era. Persp. on Polit. 8(3): 803–24. doi: 10.1017/S1537592710002045

Mettler, Suzanne, and John Sides (2012, September 24) We are the 96 percent. New York Times. Opinion Pages.

Metzenbaum, Shelly (2013) Performance management: the real research challenge. Public Admin. Rev. 73(6): 857–58. doi: 10.1111/puar.12150

Metzenbaum, Shelly (2014, September 15) Without users, performance measurement is useless. Gov. Exec. http://www.govexec.com/excellence/promising-practices/2014/09/without-users-performance-measurement-useless/94097/

Miles, Kathryn (2014, October 30) Our failing weather infrastructure. New York Times, p A31 New York print edition.

Mirowski, Philip (2015, March 14-15), [Remarks at New York City forum on] "What's wrong with the economy—and with economics?" New York Review of Books. NYR Daily. http://www.nybooks.com/daily/2015/03/29/whats-wrong-with-the-economy/

Moe, Ronald C (1994 March-April) The "Reinventing Government" exercise: misinterpreting the problem, misjudging the consequences. Public Admin. Rev. 54(2): 111–122. doi: 10.2307/976519

Moe, Ronald C, and Robert S. Gilmour (1995 March-April) Rediscovering principles of public administration: the neglected foundation of public law. Public Admin. Rev. 55(2): 135–146. doi: 10.2307/977179

Moore, Mark H (2014) Public Value accounting: establishing the philosophical basis. Public Admin. Rev. 74(4): 465–477. doi: 10.1111/puar.12198

Moss, David A (2012, September-October) interview, The other commons. Harvard Mag 115(1): 40-43, within longer feature entitled Can America compete, 26–43

Moynihan, Donald P (2008) The dynamics of performance management; constructing information and reform. Georgetown University Press, Washington DC

Moynihan, Donald P, and Stéphane Lavertu (2012) Do performance reforms change how federal managers manage? Brookings Institution, Issues in Governance Studies 52. http://www.brookings.edu/research/papers/2012/10/11-management-moynihan

Moynihan, Donald P and Joe Soss (2014, May-June) Policy feedback and the politics of administration. Public Admin. Rev. 74(3): 320–32. doi: 10.1111/puar.12200

Murray, Michael A (1975) Comparing public and private management: an exploratory essay. Public Admin. Rev. 35(4): 364–371. doi: 10.2307/974538

Musgrave, Richard A (1956/57) A multiple theory of budget determination. FinanzArchiv/Public Finance Analysis 17(3): 333–343. http://www.jstor.org/stable/40909134

Nixon, Ron (2011, September 12) Government pays more in contracts, study finds. New York Times, p A16 New York print edition. http://www.nytimes.com/2011/09/13/us/13contractor.html

Nixon, Ron (2013, February 6) Trying to stem losses, Post Office seeks to end Saturday letter delivery. New York Times, p A15 New York print edition.

Norman, Richard (2006) Managing for outcomes while accounting for outputs: redefining "public value" in New Zealand's performance management system. A paper developed for "A performing public sector", Leuven Belgium

O'Harrow, Robert, Jr. and Scott Higham (2007, May 23) Changes spurred buying, abuses. The Washington Post. http://www.washingtonpost.com/wp-dyn/content/article/2007/05/22/AR2007052201653.html

OECD (2006) Purchasing Power Parity methodological manual. Accessed November 2012. http://www.oecd.org/std/pricesandpurchasingpowerparitiesppp/37984983.pdf. Currently accessible only in a new version with substantive changes at EUROSTAT-OECD (see above)

Offe, Claus (2009) Governance: an 'empty signifier'? Constellations 16(4): 550–562. doi: 10.1111/j.1467-8675.2009.00570.x

Offe, Claus (2010, Winter) Shared social responsibility: reflections on the need for and supply of 'responsible' patterns of social reform. Transit 40: 86–104.

Offe, Claus (2012) "Shared social responsibility"– a concept in search of its political meaning and promise. In: Farrell, Gilda et al. (eds) Shared social responsibility: putting theory into practice. Trends in social cohesion, No. 24. Council of Europe Publishing, Strasbourg, pp 29–48 http://www.coe.int/t/dg3/socialpolicies/socialcohesiondev/source/Trends/Trends-24_en.pdf.

Offe, Claus (2014) "Shared social responsibility, a concept in search of its political meaning and promise. Berlin J 26 (Spring): 6–9 http://www.americanacademy.de/home/about-us/berlin-journal/issue-26-spring-2014

Offer, Avner (2002) Why has the public sector grown so large in market societies? The political economy of prudence in the UK, c. 1870-2000. Oxford Economic and Social History Working Papers, 22-W44

Offer, Avner (2012 February-March) Economics and society. The ethical dimension. World Economics Association Conferences on economics and society, and the ethical dimension.

Ogle, Greg (2000) Between statistical imperatives and theoretical obsessions. An inquiry into the definition and measurement of the economy. Dissertation, University of Adelaide. Section 1, Chapter 1, The History of "Production" http://users.senet.com.au/ ~ gregogle/PhD_home.html and also at https://digital.library.adelaide.edu.au/dspace/handle/2440/19668

Oppel, Richard A, Jr., and Abby Goodnough (2014, May 30) Doctor shortage is cited in delays at V.A. hospitals. New York Times, p A1 http://www.nytimes.com/2014/05/30/us/doctor-shortages-cited-in-va-hospital-waits.html?hp

Osborne, David (2016) Biography. Reason Foundation website. http://reason.org/authors/show/david-osborne

Osborne, David, and Ted Gaebler (1992) Reinventing government: how the entrepreneurial spirit is transforming the public sector. Addison-Wesley, Reading MA

Osborne, Stephen P. (2006) The new public governance? Public Mgmt. Rev. 8(3): 377–387. doi: 10.1080/14719030600853022

Perelman, Michael (2006) Railroading economics: the creation of the free market mythology. Monthly Review Press, New York

Perez-Johnson, Irma, and Paul Decker (2001) Customer choice or business as usual? Promoting innovation in the design of WIA training programs through the individual training account experiment. Mathematica Policy Research, Inc., Paper prepared for the National Research Conference on Workforce Security Issues in the United Stated, June 26-27, 2001, Washington, D.C.

Pierce, Olga (2009, October 20) Medicare drug planners now lobbyists, with billions at stake. ProPublica: Eye on Health Care Reform. https://www.propublica.org/article/medicare-drug-planners-now-lobbyists-with-billions-at-stake-1020

Polanyi, Karl (1944) The great transformation: the political and economic origins of our time. Beacon, Boston

Pollitt, Christopher (2007 August) The New Public Management: an overview of its current status. Revista Administraţie Şi Management Public 9: 110–115 www.ramp.ase.ro/en/_data/files/articole/8_01.pdf

Pollitt, Christopher et al. (2013) What do we know about public management reform? Concepts, models, and some approximate guidelines. Paper supporting a presentation to the conference and workshop, Towards A Comprehensive Reform of Public Governance, Lisbon, January 28-30, 2013. Online version at http://www.gulbenkian.pt/media/files/FTP_files/pdfs/CONF_Jan2013_SetorPublico/SetorPublico_28JAN_0Pollitt_paper.pdf.

Ponnuru, Ramesh, and Yuval Levin (2014, November 6) How Republicans can improve higher education. Washington Post. https://www.washingtonpost.com/opinions/how-republicans-can-improve-higher-education-and-help-the-party/2014/11/06/d82aeb02-6532-11e4-836c-83bc4f26eb67_story.html

Porter, Eduardo (2015, April 1) Tax breaks conceal gears of government. New York Times, p B1 New York print edition.

Purdy, Jedediah (2011) A foxy hedgehog: the consistent perceptions of Carol Rose. William and Mary Bill of Rights J 19: 1033–1037. http://scholarship.law.duke.edu/faculty_scholarship/2488

Pyke, Alan (2014, September 13) How some CEOs cheat their way to higher pay. ThinkProgress. http://thinkprogress.org/economy/2013/09/13/2620121/ceo-pay-performance-based-cheating/

Rabovsky, Thomas (2014 Nov.-Dec.) Support for performance-based funding. Public Admin. Rev. 74(6): 761–774. doi: 10.1111/puar.12274

Radin, Beryl A (2006) Challenging the performance movement: accountability, complexity and democratic values. Georgetown University, Washington, D.C.

Radin, Beryl A (2011a) Does performance measurement actually improve accountability? http://www.academia.edu/1566371/Does_Performance_Measurement_Actually_Improve_Accountability

Radin, Beryl A (2011b) Federalist No. 71: can the federal government be held accountable for performance? Public Admin. Rev. 71(suppl.1): s128-s134. doi: 10.1111/j.1540-6210.2011.02472.x

Radin, Beryl A (2012) Federal management reform in a world of contradictions. Georgetown University, Washington, D.C.

Rainey, Hal G, and Young Han Chun (2007, online 2009) Public and private management compared. In: Ferlie, Ewan, et al. (Eds) Oxford handbook of public management. doi: 10.1093/oxfordhb/9780199226443.003.0005 http://www.oxfordhandbooks.com/view/10.1093/oxfordhb/9780199226443.001.0001/oxfordhb-9780199226443-e-5

Ranson, Stewart, and John Stewart (1989) Citizenship and government: the challenge for management in the public domain. Polit. Stud. 37(1): 5–24. doi: 10.1111/j.1467-9248.1989.tb00262.x

Ranson, Stewart, and John Stewart (1994) Management for the public domain; enabling the learning society. St. Martin's, New York

Reed, Lawrence W (1983, June 1) [Review of Privatizing the public sector: how to shrink government, by E. S. Savas.] FEE: Foundation for Economic Education. http://fee.org/articles/book-review-privatizing-the-public-sector-how-to-shrink-government-by-e-s-savas/

Reinhardt, Uwe E (2010, August 20) Is "more efficient" always better? New York Times Economix section. http://economix.blogs.nytimes.com/2010/08/20/is-more-efficient-always-better/

Reynolds, Gillian, and C. Eugene Steuerle (2009) Tax expenditures: why are they controversial? Tax Policy Center (Urban Institute and Brookings Institution), Tax Policy Briefing Book. http://www.taxpolicycenter.org/briefing-book/background/expenditures/controversial.cfm

Rhodes, R A W, and John Wanna (27, November 8) The limits to public value or rescuing responsible government from the Platonic Guardians. Austral J of Public Admin. 66(4): 406–421 10.1111/j.1467-8500.2007.00553.x

Rivkin, Jan W, Michael E Porter, Rosabeth Moss Kanter and David A Moss (2012 September-October), interviews within feature article, Can America compete? Harvard Mag 115(1): 26–43. http://harvardmagazine.com/2012/09/can-america-compete

Rose, Carol M. (1986) The comedy of the commons: commerce, custom, and inherently public property. University of Chicago Law Review 53(3): 711–81. Republished as Yale Faculty Scholarship Series, Paper 1828. http://digitalcommons.law.yale.edu/fss_papers/1828

Rosenbaum, Allan (2014a) Have public administrators (and the discipline of public administration) failed our nation? Public Admin. Times 37(2): 9–10

Rosenbaum, Allan (2014b October) The myth of public sector failure and incompetence: who benefits, how and why? Public Admin. Times 37(3): 3–13

Rosta, Miklós (2011) What makes a New Public Management reform successful? An institutional analysis. Maxwell School of Citizenship and Public Affairs, Syracuse University. https://www.maxwell.syr.edu/search.aspx?q=rosta

Sachs, Jeffrey D (2013, March 31) On the economy, think long-term. New York Times, p A19 New York print edition for April 1. http://www.nytimes.com/2013/04/01/opinion/on-the-economy-think-long-term.html

Sachs, Jeffrey D (2014, November 25) Sustainable development economics. Project Syndicate http://www.project-syndicate.org/commentary/promote-sustainable-development-economics-by-jeffrey-d-sachs-2014-11

Salzman, Randy (2014, October 16) A blueprint for bankruptcy. TruthOut. http://www.truth-out.org/news/item/26848-a-blueprint-for-bankruptcy

Schuck, Peter H (2014) Why government fails so often, and how it can do better. Princeton University, Princeton

Sclar, Elliott D (2000) You don't always get what you pay for: the economics of privatization. Cornell University, Ithaca.

Segal, David (2012, June 23) A Georgia town takes the People's business private. New York Times, p BU1 of New York print edition for June 24. http://www.nytimes.com/2012/06/24/business/a-georgia-town-takes-the-peoples-business-private.html?

Sekera, June (2014, July 9) Rethinking the definition of "public goods." Real-World Econ. Rev. Blog. https://rwer.wordpress.com/?s=sekera

Shapiro, Joseph (2014, May 19) As court fees rise, the poor are paying the price. National Public Radio, News Investigations, with update on May 23. http://www.npr.org/2014/05/19/312158516/increasing-court-fees-punish-the-poor

Shear, Michael (2015, September 12) With website to research colleges, Obama abandons ranking system. New York Times

Shionoya, Yuichi (2005) The soul of the German Historical School; methodological essays on Schmoller, Weber, and Schumpeter. Springer, Boston

Siltala, Juha (2013) New public management: the evidence-based worst practice? Admin. 45(4): 468–493. doi:10.1177/0095399713483385

Simon, Herbert A (1997) Administrative behavior: a study of decision-making processes in administrative organization. 3rd edition, Free Press, New York

Sirota, David (2013, May 21) Anyone regret slashing National Weather Service budget now? Salon. http://www.salon.com/2013/05/21/how_are_we_cutting_the_weather_service_now/

Slaughter, Sheila,and Larry L. Leslie (1997) Academic capitalism: politics, policies, and the entrepreneurial university. Johns Hopkins University, Baltimore.

Slaughter, Sheila, and Gary Rhoades (2004) Academic capitalism in the new economy: markets, state and higher education. Johns Hopkins University, Baltimore.

Smith, Adam (2013) Adam Smith on the functions of government. Republic of Lagrangia webposting April 6, excerpting Smith's (1776) An Inquiry into the Nature and Causes of the Wealth of Nations (version online at Project Gutenberg). http://republicoflagrangia.org/2013/04/06/adam-smith-on-the-functions-of-government/

Smith, Thomas A (2014) [Review of Why government fails so often, by Peter Schuck and Simeon E. Baldwin.] Yale Alumni Mag. 77(6): 58 https://yalealumnimagazine.com/articles/3936/reviews

Stewart, John, interviewed by Liza Donaldson (1994, March 5) Professor drives another lesson home in quest for accountability. Independent (UK) http://www.independent.co.uk/news/education/education-news/professor-drives-another-lesson-home-in-quest-for-accountability-birmingham-universitys-quango-critic-has-a-way-of-touching-off-debate-liza-donaldson-explains-1427358.html

Stiglitz, Joseph E (1988) Economics of the public sector. 2nd edn. W W Norton, New York

Stiglitz, Joseph E (2000) Economics of the public sector. 3rd edn. W W Norton, New York

Stillman, Sarah (2014, June 23) Get out of jail inc. New Yorker. http://www.newyorker.com/magazine/2014/06/23/get-out-of-jail-inc

Stone, Christopher (2013, April 2) False economies, Part 1: decoding efficiency. Centre for Policy Development. https://cpd.org.au/2013/04/decoding-efficiency/

Storm, Servaas, interview by Lynn Stuart Parramore (2015, January 9) Welcome to the European Hunger Games, brought to you by mainstream economics. Truth-Out. http://www.truth-out.org/news/item/28449-welcome-to-the-european-hunger-games-brought-to-you-by-mainstream-economics

Story, Louise (2012a, December 1) As companies seek tax deals, governments pay high price. New York Times http://www.nytimes.com/2012/12/02/us/how-local-taxpayers-bankroll-corporations.html?pagewanted=all

Story, Louise (2012b, December 2) Lines blur as Texas gives industries a bonanza. New York Times

Story, Louise (2012c, December 3) Michigan town woos Hollywood, but ends up with a bit part. New York Times,

Stretton, Hugh, and Lionel Orchard (1994) Public goods, public enterprise, public choice – the theoretical foundations for the contemporary attack on government. St. Martin's, New York

Studenski, Paul (1939, November) Government as a producer. Annals of the Amer. Acad. of Political and Social. Sci. [issue on government expansion in the economic sphere], 206: 23–34. www.jstor.org/stable/1022414

Studenski, Paul (1958) The income of nations. New York University, New York

Talburt, Susan (2005) [Review of Academic capitalism and the new economy: markets, state, and higher education, by Sheila Slaughter and Gary Rhoades.] Rev. of Higher Educ. 28(4): 638–640. https://muse.jhu.edu/journals/review_of_higher_education/v028/28.4talburt.html

Taleb, Nassim Nicholas (2010), The black swan: the impact of the highly improbable. 2nd edn. Random House, New York

Tankersley, William (2014, September/October) [Review of From pleasure machines to moral communities, by Geoffrey Hodgson]. Public Admin Rev 74(5): 671–75

Teachout, Zephyr (2014) Corruption in America: from Benjamin Franklin's snuff box to Citizens United. Harvard University Press, Cambridge MA

Teles, Steven M (2013) Kludgeocracy in America. National Affairs 17: 97–114 http://www.nationalaffairs.com/publications/detail/kludgeocracy-in-america

Tritten, Travis J (2014, August 5).VA reform bill preserves employee bonuses. Stars and Stripes. http://www.stripes.com/news/veterans/va-reform-bill-preserves-employee-bonuses-1.296911

U.S. Department of Treasury, Office of Economic Policy (2014, September) Expanding our nation's infrastructure through innovative financing. Washington, D.C. https://www.treasury.gov/about/organizational-structure/offices/Pages/Economic-Policy.aspx

Ubel, Peter A, and Susan Door Goold (1998) "Rationing" health care: not all definitions are created equal. Arch Intern Med 158(3): 209–214. doi:10.1001/archinte.158.3.209

Upbin, Bruce (2013, June 13) Debunking the narrative of Silicon Valley's innovation might. Forbes.

Verkuil, Paul R (2007) Outsourcing sovereignty: why privatization of government functions threatens democracy and what we can do about it. Cambridge University, Cambridge

Volcker, Paul (2014) Vision without execution is hallucination. Public Admin. Rev. 74(4): 439–441. doi: 10.1111/puar.12239

Wall Street Journal Review and Outlook (2014, May 29). The VA's bonus culture: how senior Veterans Affairs officials get paid more for lack of performance. Wall Street J. http://www.wsj.com/articles/the-vas-bonus-culture-1401406048

Wandschneider, Philip R (1994) [Review of The economics of collective choice by Joe B Stevens.] Amer. Journal of . Agric. Econ. 76(3): 686–688

Warner, Marina (2015) Learning my lesson. London Rev. Books 37(6): 8–14

Warner, Mildred (2011, April 4) The pendulum swings again. New York Times, Opinion Pages http://www.nytimes.com/roomfordebate/2011/04/03/is-privatization-a-bad-deal-for-cities-and-states/the-pendulum-swings-again

Warren, Paul (2005) Key Indicators in Canada. Statistics Canada, Economic Analysis Research Paper Series, Catalog No. 11F0027MIE — No. 037 http://publications.gc.ca/site/archivee-archived.html?url=http://publications.gc.ca/Collection/Statcan/11F0027M/11F0027MIE2005037.pdf

Weber, Max (1919) Politics as a vocation. Second lecture in a series delivered to Free Students Union of Bavaria, Munich, January 28, 1919. Published as Politik als Beruf. Available online in English translation thru Wikisource.

Wedel, Janine, and Linda Keenan (2010, September 2) Shadow elite: selling out Uncle Sam; government contracting - a free market farce. Huffpost Politics. http://www.huffingtonpost.com/janine-r-wedel/emshadow-eliteem-selling_b_703127.html

Weigelt, Matthew (2013, January 3) GSA: expand fee program. Federal Computer Week (=FCW). https://fcw.com/articles/2013/01/03/gsa-fee.aspx

Weinstein, Michael M (2009, December 14) Paul A. Samuelson, economist, dies at 94. New York Times, p A1 of New York print edition http://www.nytimes.com/2009/12/14/business/economy/14samuelson.html?pagewanted=all

Weisbrod, Burton A. (1964) External Benefits of Public Education; An Economic Analysis. Princeton University, Princeton

Wentzel, Arnold (2011?) Market vs state is the wrong debate. Academia.edu, undated talk. http://www.academia.edu/3454889/Market_versus_state_is_the_wrong_debate

White House, Office of Domestic Policy, press release (1993, March 3) A revolution in government. http://clinton6.nara.gov/1993/03/1993-03-03-a-revolution-in-government-office-of-domestic-policy.html

Wikipedia entry: Tax Expenditure (2015, last modified August 3). http://en.wikipedia.org/wiki/Tax_expenditure

Williams, Timothy (2014, August 17) Seeking new start, finding steep cost: Workforce Investment Act leaves many jobless and in debt. New York Times, p A1 of New York print edition, August 18. http://www.nytimes.com/2014/08/18/us/workforce-investment-act-leaves-many-jobless-and-in-debt.html?module=Search&mabReward=relbias:w,{&_r=0

Wilson, James Q (1989) Bureaucracy: what government agencies do and why they do it. Basic Books, New York

Wilson, Richard Clay (2013) Rethinking public administration: the case for management. Melvin & Leigh, Irvine CA

Wolff, Robert (2010) Collective choice theory first installment. http://robert-wolff.blogspot.de/2010/07/collective-choice-theory-first.html

Wong, Edward (2013, April 22) In China, breathing becomes a childhood risk. New York Times, p A1 of New York print edition, April 23. http://www.nytimes.com/2013/04/23/world/asia/pollution-is-radically-changing-childhood-in-chinas-cities.html

Wuyts, Marc (1992) Deprivation and public need. In: Macintosh, Maureen and Marc Wuyts (eds) Development policy and public action. Oxford University, Oxford, p 13–38

Index

© June A. Sekera 2016
J.A. Sekera, *The Public Economy in Crisis*,
SpringerBriefs in Economics, DOI 10.1007/978-3-319-40487-5

27517410R00086

Printed in Poland
by Amazon Fulfillment
Poland Sp. z o.o., Wrocław